Musical Instruments You Can Make

Musical Instruments You Can Make

Hugh Garnett

Pitman Publishing

First published 1976

PITMAN PUBLISHING LTD
Pitman House, 39 Parker Street, London WC 2B 5PB, UK

PITMAN MEDICAL PUBLISHING CO LTD
42 Camden Road, Tunbridge Wells, Kent TN 1 2QD, UK

FOCAL PRESS LTD
31 Fitzroy Square, London W 1P, 6BH, UK

PITMAN PUBLISHING CORPORATION
6 East 43 Street, New York, NY 10017, USA

FEARON PUBLISHERS INC
6 Davis Drive, Belmont, California 94002, USA

PITMAN PUBLISHING PTY LTD
Pitman House, 158 Bouverie Street, Carlton, Victoria 3053, Australia

PITMAN PUBLISHING
COPP CLARK PUBLISHING
517 Wellington Street West, Toronto M5V 1G 1, Canada

SIR ISAAC PITMAN AND SONS LTD
Banda Street, PO Box 46038, Nairobi, Kenya

PITMAN PUBLISHING CO SA (PTY) LTD
Craighall Mews, Jan Smuts Avenue, Craighall Park, Johannesburg 2001, South Africa

ISBN 0 273 00727 0

Text set in 11/12 pt. Photon Imprint, printed by photolithography, and bound in Great Britain at The Pitman Press, Bath

G14:16

Contents

Preface

After many years of experience, working with children, and as a hobby, inventing and making musical instruments from scrap and other unlikely materials, I have come to realize that the results do not always have to be primitive, or merely toy versions of the real thing. I have also found that instruments of a surprisingly high quality can be made for remarkably little cost. The secret lies in seeing the possibilities in everyday materials, and in finding neat and practical solutions to seemingly awkward problems.

So the instruments described in this book may seem a little unusual at first—in fact they are all in some way original—but they still belong to one or other of the families of bangers, twangers and blowers which have been popular for centuries. Where they are different is in their methods of construction, suggested by modern materials not available to our forefathers, such as fast-setting epoxy adhesives, plastic water piping which will take screw-threads, tough synthetic fabrics, and perpetually springy plywood. Much of the delight

to be had in making the instruments comes from discovering what can be done with these and other materials.

Almost everything you need can be obtained from local shops and builders' merchants. Some of the instruments are really very easy to make, and even the more difficult ones are within the scope of a reasonably competent handyman. Perhaps enthusiastic readers will be encouraged to go on experimenting for themselves on the lines suggested here. Maybe then they will experience, as I have done, something of the thrill which our ancestors must have felt when they were first inventing musical instruments.

A word of caution: with a book like this, full of photographs and drawings, there is always a temptation to wade straight in, without really studying the instructions. Those who do may soon find themselves out of their depth. I have learned the hard way. I hope this book will help to make it easy for you.

H.G.

1 Tools, adhesives and materials

The experienced handyman will probably already possess most of the necessary tools. Here, for the beginner, is a list of useful items:

> Miniature hacksaw
> Light hammer
> Stanley knife
> Scissors
> Pliers
> Assorted small files, including a 'mousetail' file
> Small, medium and large screwdrivers
> Three or four 'G' cramps
> Hand drill, with twist bits from $\frac{1}{16}$ in. to $\frac{1}{4}$ in., and countersink bit
> Various grades of abrasive paper, mainly medium and fine.

For the larger instruments, some ordinary woodworking tools will be needed, including a smoothing plane, chisels, spokeshave, sharpening stone, panel and tenon saws, carpenter's square, and a marking gauge, or better still, a cutting gauge.

A work bench fitted with an engineer's vice as well as a woodworking vice would be a great asset. However, it is quite possible to make the simpler instruments on a kitchen table, using a bench hook, preferably clamped to the table.

Bench hook

This almost indispensible item can be easily made using three small offcuts of wood from a timber yard or a building site. As its name implies, it hooks, either way up, over the edge of a bench or table. The work to be supported, for sawing, drilling, etc., is pressed firmly into the angle formed by the two upper pieces of wood.

A useful size for the bench hook is about 8 in. by 5 in. (20 cm by 30 cm), the wood being from $\frac{3}{4}$ in. to 1 in. thick (2 cm to 2·5 cm). It can be nailed and glued together. Fig. 2 shows how two 'G' cramps and a bench hook can take the place of a vice if both hands are needed, as for instance when drilling a hole in a piece of plastic piping.

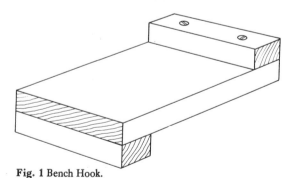

Fig. 1 Bench Hook.

Useful adhesives

Hardware shops stock an ever increasing range of adhesives, suitable for a variety of purposes. These are some of the most useful:

Fig. 2 A piece of plastic pipe firmly held for drilling, using a
bench hook and two 'G' cramps.

Epoxy and Polymer Adhesives

  Araldite Rapid (very strong—ideal for small
    joints in almost anything)
  Bostik Quick Set Polyurethane Adhesive
    (immensely strong)

Woodworking Adhesives

  Cascamite (extremely strong)
  Evo-stik Resin W (convenient to use)

General Purpose Adhesives

  Bostik Clear Adhesive 1 (for glueing fabrics to
    wood etc.)
  Contact adhesives (various). There are several
    makes on the market. Some set harder than
    others. They are very useful for joining large
    surfaces together, but are often liable to
    'creep', especially when too near a source of
    heat.
  Copydex (a rubbery glue developed for carpets
    and fabrics—excellent for making drum-
    heads)

Wood

New timber is very expensive, as well as being
liable to shrink and split. Timber yards usually
stock Ramin, an imported semi-hardwood which
is quite reliable and easy to work with. If it has a
straight and even grain, and is fairly dense, it can
be a useful substitute for some of the more expensive hardwoods.

Reclaimed wood, provided it is free from active
woodworm or dry rot, is generally better than new
wood for making instruments, being thoroughly
seasoned. A possible source of oak and beech is old
school furniture, which is sometimes disposed of
cheaply.

Gaboon plywood, which is in plentiful supply, is
suitable for making sound-boards and sound
boxes. Gaboon is a kind of soft mahogany, with a
pleasant grain and colour. Marine-quality
plywood, for boat building, is more expensive and
less resonant, and should therefore be avoided.

When buying new wood, hardboard or plastic
laminates, it is a good idea to search among the
offcuts, which are normally sold much more cheaply than cut sizes.

Other materials

Details of what is required are given in the appropriate chapters. Nails and screws, nuts and
bolts, and copper draught-excluders are sold by
hardware shops and tool-merchants. Whitworth
threads are specified for bolts needing wing-nuts,
since these do not seem to be made with any other
threads. Plastic waste piping is usually stocked
by builders' merchants in their plumbing
departments. There are several different makes,
sizes and colours on the market, so it is worth
trying more than one, especially if you want contrasting colours.

PVC adhesive tape is sold by most radio and
television shops; being fairly easily stretched, it is
useful for binding curved surfaces.

Fabric-backed adhesive tape, sold by most
stationers in several different widths, is far
stronger than PVC tape, but is inelastic.

Some shops stock a wide variety of makes,
qualities and widths of binding tape. The more
expensive brands are generally more durable.

Steel guitar strings, suitable for the dulcimer
and the psalteries, are sold by most music shops.

Leather, sufficiently hard for plectrum making,
may sometimes be cut from an old leather belt, but
failing this, sole and heel leather from shoe
repairers may be used.

Reclaimed materials

Lastly, but by no means least, do not disdain to
search rubbish tips. I found in one such tip enough
well-seasoned beechwood from an old bunk bed to
make the key coverings, hitch-pin rails and wrest
planks for several keyed psalteries.

Measurements—Metric and Imperial

At the time of writing we are poised rather uncom-
fortably between the two systems. The policy
adopted in this book is therefore as follows:

All drilling sizes are given as fractions of an inch,
since not all hardware shops stock metric drills.

Measurements which are not absolutely critical
are usually given in both forms.

Small and exact measurements are given in the
metric form. We have, after all, had metric scales
on our rulers for many years. Opposite are some
reasonably accurate comparisons.

Table of Metric Equivalents

1 yard		91·5 cm
1 foot		30·5 cm
1 inch	(slightly more than)	2·5 cm

Standard thicknesses of plywood:

12 mm	$\frac{1}{2}$ inch
9 mm	$\frac{3}{8}$ inch
6 mm	$\frac{1}{4}$ inch
4 mm	$\frac{3}{16}$ inch
3 mm	$\frac{1}{8}$ inch

2 Drums

Since before recorded history, drums have been associated with ritual and magic, and this feeling still lurks not far below the surface. Almost any hollow object may serve as a drum. The sound produced will vary greatly according to the shape and size of the resonating space, and the resilience of the material, not only of the drum itself, but also of the implement with which it is beaten or struck.

Objects needing little or no modification for use as drums

(a) *Inflated rubber objects*, such as balloons, beach balls, football bladders and space-hoppers, held by the neck, valve, or any other protruding part, and tapped with the hand, or with a wooden spoon.

(b) *Hollow objects* of wood or plastic.

(c) *Plastic containers* from food stores, such as cheese, yoghurt and margarine pots, washing-up liquid and bleach containers, or any other fairly rigid containers made from thin plastic. When they have been washed and dried, some will sound more reasonant with the lids left on, especially those which are shaped like flower pots. Owing to their conical shape, these will often produce a note of definite pitch when tapped on one end, and a different note from the opposite end. Cylindrical containers, open at one end, may be tuned experimentally by cutting them down to various lengths. They are quite easy to cut with kitchen scissors. A group of players with an assortment of

these can produce some interesting pitched percussive effects, using the fingers, the non-pointed ends of knitting needles, or thin pieces of wood, as beaters.

(d) *Wooden or plastic coke-hods*, inverted, held between the knees or under one arm, and tapped on the end, using either the flattened hand, or one or other of the beaters described on pp. 16–17. (When using an old hod remember to clean it out first.)

(e) *Plastic buckets and waste bins* can be used in a similar way. Some will sound much better than others.

Single headed drums using cardboard tubes

Certain items supplied to schools and offices, such as maps, charts and posters, are packed in strong cardboard tubes with plastic caps. By removing one cap, and tapping the other one, these can often be made to work quite well as drums just as they are.

Tubes of this type may be anything from $1\frac{1}{2}$ to 4 in. in diameter. The larger ones are more effective as drums. With both caps removed, some suitable material can be stretched tightly over one end. This is less difficult, using such a relatively narrow tube, than with a wider drum. A definite pitch may also be established, which can be raised by shortening the tube, as well as by tightening the head. Long tubes can be sawn into two or more pieces to make drums. A length of 18 in. or more is

Fig. 3 (*left*) Glass-fibre drum on a cardboard tube, before trimming and decorating; (*right*) Bath hat drum with cardboard tube.

needed to give a really deep tone.

The drum-head may be made from:

(a) *A rubber bathing cap*, with the straps removed, pulled hard down, and secured by looping several large rubber bands around the tube. This will produce a rather dull but very deep tone, best heard from the direction of the open end.

The head will need to be pulled tight from time to time.

(b) *A bath hat*, secured with ½ in. wide rayon elastic. Choose one of the tougher kinds of bath hat from Boots' or Woolworth's. Place it centrally over the drum, and bind about a yard of the rayon elastic fairly tightly round it near the top of the drum, as many times as it will go. The first end of the elastic should be left projecting, so that it can be stapled or sewn to its other end when the binding is completed. Now work carefully round, pulling the bath hat as tight as possible. The pressure built up by elastic binding is very considerable, for which reason it is dangerous to wrap it around any part of the body. However, if the drumhead still seems to slacken in use, more elastic can be added.

A brightly coloured bath hat, on a painted tube, will make a decorative-looking drum.

(c) *David's Isopon resin* (or equivalent), and glass-fibre matting. This is particularly suitable for drums with a diameter of 6 in. or more, whether made from cardboard tubes, or from wooden or metal containers. It is extremely tough, and produces a penetrating 'stacatto' sound, not to everybody's taste, but one which can certainly be heard.

The material is sold at most garages and car accessory shops, and is the same as that used for making glass fibre boat hulls. Be sure to buy the liquid resin and hardener, not the paste filler, and read the instructions carefully. Stand the drum on a piece of newspaper to protect the table or bench from drops of resin. Cut a circle of glass-fibre matting (coarse for larger drums, fine 'surface tissue' for smaller ones), about 4 in. larger in diameter than the drum, and place it centrally on the top. Secure it very gently with small pieces of adhesive tape, just below the rim of the drum, at intervals all the way round. Do not attempt to pull it tight, as it will tear very easily.

Then mix a small quantity of resin and hardener, the equivalent of about three tablespoonfuls, in the proportions specified by the manufacturer, and spread it very gently with a small paste brush or spatula, over the top, and around the rim for a width of about half an inch. After twenty minutes or so, when this has 'cured' to a state of semi-rigidity, add a further layer of glass fibre matting, and repeat the process. The more layers you add, the tougher the drum will become, but it will sound better if left fairly thin. A 6 in. (15 cm) diameter drum works well with only three layers of the thinnest surface tissue. A 10 in. diameter drum would need four layers.

The plastic will take a few hours to cure completely, after which the untreated edges of the glass matting can be cut away, and any rough places smoothed with a coarse file. This drum can be decorated in any number of ways, remembering that a wooden or cardboard tube will need coating with a sealer, such as emulsion paint, before applying gloss paint.

Drums which can play tunes

A popular way to make drums used to be by lacing pieces of rubber from old inner tubes over the ends of large tin cans. This was resonant and effective while it lasted, but the lacing holes soon tore out, and in any case real rubber inner tubes are now virtually unobtainable. Synthetic ones sound very dull.

The situation calls for what the experts now like to term 'lateral thinking'. Put plainly, this means that, since no amount of pondering on the excellence of genuine rubber inner tubes will bring them back, we have to think of something else. With the necessary qualities of toughness, lightness and elasticity in view, I experimented by treating various fabrics with almost every type of glue on the market. One combination proved more successful than any other. This was Copydex adhesive spread on both sides of lightweight Tricel fabric, of the sort used for making shirts and blouses. Other synthetic fabrics are almost as good, but Tricel is tougher than most.

Copydex is a flexible, rubbery adhesive, developed for sticking carpets and fabrics. It dries to a drab, yellowish colour, but on strongly coloured fabrics this hardly shows. It shrinks slightly on drying, and, once dry, is quite impervious to atmospheric conditions. The resulting material is so tough and flexible that it can be used to make a rather interesting and unusual kind of drum, sometimes referred to as a 'talking' drum.

The 'talking' drum is double-skinned, and shaped like an hour-glass. It occurs in Africa, from Sierra Leone to the Cameroons, and north of the Zambesi. It can also be found in Asia, as far east as Japan. It is made and played in various ways. One way is to hold it under the arm, and squeeze the lacing, thereby tightening the skins, and making possible a whole range of different pitches.

Fig. 4 The shell of the small hour-glass drum, showing the two flower pots bolted and taped together.

Small hour-glass drum

The shell

For the body, or 'shell', you will need two plastic flower pots, with 7 in. diameter rims. These pots usually have a slight dome in the centre of their base, surrounded by several drainage holes. Clean out any excess plastic from the holes, and saw off the projecting parts of the bases, on which the pots were meant to stand.

Place the two pots base to base, so that their drainage holes coincide, and bind two or three layers of PVC adhesive tape around them to fasten them together. The holes must coincide so that they allow fluctuations of air pressure to be transmitted from one end of the drum to the other.

Drill a $\frac{1}{4}$ in. hole through the centre of the bases, and bolt the pots together, using a $\frac{1}{4}$ in. nut and bolt with flat washers. Tighten the nut and bolt until the dome-shaped centres of the bases are forced together. To brighten up the rather dull brown appearance of the flower pots, the whole of the outsides can be bound with coloured PVC tape. Smooth any rough places on the tops of the rims, and the shell is now ready.

The drum heads

Each head consists of two plywood hoops, 4 mm thick, with a piece of lightweight Tricel fabric clamped between them, and treated with Copydex adhesive.

Draw four circles on the plywood, 10 in. or 25 cm in diameter. Inside each one, draw a smaller circle, $8\frac{1}{4}$ in. (21 cm) in diameter, with the same centre. The hoops can be cut out with a fretsaw by inserting the blade through a small hole for the inside cut. Alternatively, for a very neat and accurate job, use a modified cutting gauge, as described in Chapter 6 for cutting the hole in the soundboard of a psaltery. If the hoops are to be painted or varnished, it will be easier to do so at this stage rather than later.

Spread Copydex adhesive over the whole of one side of one hoop. Notice carefully the direction of the visible, or surface grain of the plywood. Lay the piece of Tricel fabric on the hoop, pulling it out evenly all round. Spread Copydex on one side of the second hoop, and place it on top of the first one, so that the fabric is sandwiched between the two. *Make certain that the surface grain of the second hoop is at right-angles to that of the first one.* If the grain of each hoop runs in the same direction, the strength will not be evenly distributed around the drum, and the hoops will then become distorted, and might break.

Align the hoops carefully, and fasten them together with sixteen panel pins, spaced opposite each other by dividing the circumference into halves, quarters, eighths and finally sixteenths. Use the excess fabric to pull the skin fairly tight on opposite sides as you go, leaving no slack places or wrinkles.

Since the panel pins will project on the other side, they should be hammered only part way in at first, and finally, hammered right in between the jaws of a vice, or over the edge of a spare piece of

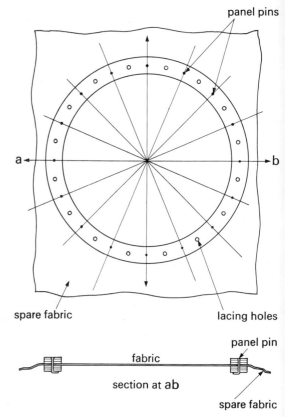

Fig. 5 Small hour-glass drum: (*above*) Drum head, spacing of holes; (*below*) Section at a–b.

wood. The hoops are then inverted, and the ends of the pins bent over and hammered down firmly.

When all is secure, place a 'blob' of Copydex adhesive (about one dessertspoonful) in the centre of one side, and spread it evenly, right into the edges of the hoop. If this is done with a plastic comb, such as hardware shops supply with contact adhesive, or for spreading tile cement, attractive wavy patterns can be made. Spread more Copydex in the same way on the reverse side, and then support the head horizontally and put in a warm place to dry. If left in the cold, it may take several days, but in an airing cupboard, it should dry overnight.

When the Copydex has set, it may still feel tacky. To cure this, brush a little talcum powder on both sides of the skin. By this time it should have tightened sufficiently to sound fairly impressive, even without the rest of the drum. Trim off the spare fabric from around the outer edge, and then make the second head in exactly the same way as the first one.

Lacing

Drill $\frac{3}{16}$ in. holes, spaced midway between the panel pins. Thread $\frac{1}{8}$ in. nylon cord through the holes, binding it over the outer edge of the hoop, as shown in Fig. 6, and knot the ends with a reef knot, which can be secured with Copydex.

Dust a little talcum powder on the rims of the flower pots, stand the drum shell centrally on one of the heads, and place the other one on the top. Fig. 6 shows how the heads are laced together. For this you will need about eleven more yards of $\frac{1}{8}$ in. nylon cord. A small piece of PVC tape, bound tightly round the end, will make the threading easier.

Pull the lacing just tight enough to keep the drum heads well in place, but not any tighter. Knot the ends together, and bind them with white PVC tape. The drum may now be tested. Hold it under one arm, and try playing it on different parts of its head, with various beaters, or with the fingertips. Squeeze the lacing with the arm, side and hand, as evenly as possible all round, to produce changes of pitch.

Tuning with a toggle

This drum is easily tuned to any pitch within its range, as follows: tie a piece of nylon cord round its waist, like a loose girdle, and insert a toggle of thin wood, about 5 in. long. Twist this, to tighten the girdle to the required amount, and insert the toggle through the lacing to hold it in position. To make the drum 'talk' again, merely loosen the girdle—it need not be removed.

Larger (bass) hour-glass drum

The shell for this consists of a plywood frame, bolted together, and bound with adhesive tape. Twelve strips of plywood, 17 in. long, 1 in. wide and $\frac{1}{4}$ in. thick (43 cm by 2·5 cm by 6 mm) are bolted to a pair of 10 in. (25 cm) hoops to form a cylinder. The strips are cut across the surface grain of the plywood, so that they will bend fairly easily. The hoops which form the rims of the shell can be salvaged from an old toy drum. If a suitable drum cannot be found, they can be made from two

Fig. 6 Small hour-glass drum complete, with tuning toggle.

strips of plywood similar to the others, likewise cut across the surface grain, each $32\frac{1}{2}$ in. (83 cm) long, and 1 in. (2·5 cm) wide. The ends are tapered as shown in Fig. 8(a).

To bend the rims into shape, immerse the plywood a little at a time in boiling water, and curve it gently, taking care not to break the wood. A pair of old gloves will protect your hands, but there is no need for them to go into the boiling water. However, children under the age of fifteen are advised not to attempt this by themselves.

Form the strip into a circle, with an overlap of about three or four inches. This can be done by bending it round a pot or pan of rather less than 10 in. in diameter. Bind the ends together for the time being, and leave the rim to dry. When ready, secure the joint with woodworking glue and a pair of panel pins, the ends of which are bent over and hammered down. Make sure first that the ends of the strip are not out of line, and that the overlap is now $1\frac{1}{8}$ in. or 3 cm. Smooth, and slightly round off the edges of the rim with glasspaper, paying special attention to the joint, to avoid abrasing or distortion of the drum head.

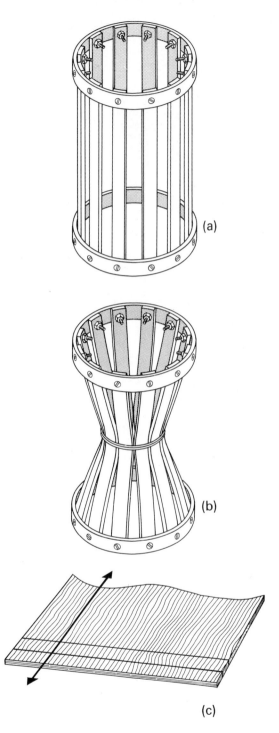

(a)

(b)

(c)

Fig. 7 Large hour-glass drum: (a) the frame of the shell bolted loosely together; (b) binding the centre to form the hour-glass shape; (c) direction of surface grain of plywood.

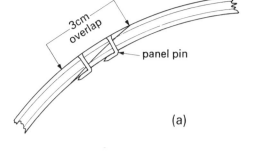

(a)

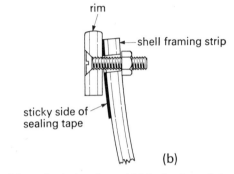

(b)

Fig. 8 Large hour-glass drum: (a) joint in plywood rim; (b) section of bolted joint.

The rims are next marked for twelve equally spaced $\frac{3}{16}$ in. holes. The first one should go through the centre of the overlapped joint, so that the nut and bolt will help to strengthen the joint. As a guide for spacing the other holes, it is useful to remember that half the radius of a circle can be stepped off twelve times around its circumference. The holes will in fact be $2\frac{1}{2}$ in. (6·4 cm) apart (measured in a straight line, *not* round the outside of the curve). The outer sides of the holes should be recessed with a countersink tool or bit, to take $\frac{3}{16}$ in. countersunk bolts. Make sure that all the holes are drilled in the centre of the width of the rim.

The straight strips should now have slightly larger ($\frac{1}{4}$ in.) holes drilled in them, with their centres $\frac{3}{8}$ in. (1 cm) from each end. The holes are made this size to allow for the slope of the ends, when the hour-glass shape is formed, and to allow for any small irregularities in the rims. (Fig. 8(b).)

Bolt the frame loosely together in the form of a cylinder. To give it an hour-glass shape, tie some string tightly round at the centre, pulling in the plywood strips until they touch each other. Check

Fig. 9 The shell of the large hour-glass drum, showing how the frame is bolted to the rims, and bound with adhesive tape.

that the whole frame is symmetrical, and not lop-sided or twisted spirally. Bind it tightly for a little way on each side of the string with PVC adhesive tape. Remove the string, and fill in the centre gap with more tape. Spread some woodworking glue round the inside of the waist to strengthen it.

Next, to form a seal at the top under the rims, undo each bolt in turn, and work all round, inserting fabric-backed adhesive tape, at least 1 in. wide, *sticky side outwards*, between the rims and the framing strips. Double-sided masking tape will work even better. Prick holes for the bolts in the tape, and make vertical cuts in it, one below each bolt hole, to allow for the slope of the sides, otherwise wrinkles will form in the tape. Stick the tape firmly all round the inside of the rim, near the top. Replace each bolt as you go, tightening it from the outside with a screwdriver, sufficiently to spring the wood a little, but not enough to break it. The nuts will begin to bite into the wood, and thereby lock themselves in position. Finally, continue the external binding, with PVC tape, until it overlaps as much as possible of the fabric or masking tape under the rims. The whole thing will be stronger with two, or even three layers of external binding. Make sure that the ends of the side frames are below the top edges of the rims, so that they do not touch the drum heads.

The drum heads

These are made in the same way as for the smaller hour-glass drum, but have more lacing holes. The hoops are cut from $\frac{1}{4}$ in. or 6 mm plywood, with an external diameter of 12 in. or 30·5 cm, and an internal diameter of $10\frac{1}{2}$ in. or 26·5 cm. There are 24 panel pins and lacing holes, which are spaced by

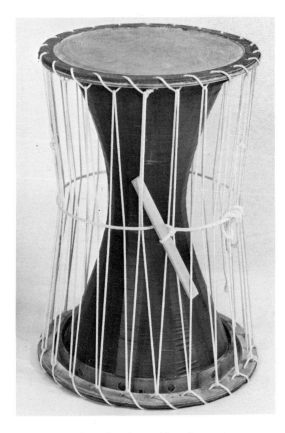

Fig. 10 Large hour-glass drum with tuning toggle.

stepping off half the radius around the circumference, and dividing each segment once more. For the lacing, you will need about 24 yards of $\frac{1}{8}$ in. nylon cord.

Two-ply heads, made by clamping one extra piece of Tricel fabric between the hoops, will give a slightly duller sound, but are extremely durable and tough.

This drum, like the smaller one, can be tuned with a girdle and toggle. It can be hung on a cord round the neck, and played with one hand at each end. A pair, tuned a fourth or a fifth apart, can be used like timpani. A skilful player can keep the drum in tune with other instruments by squeezing it under one arm.

Beaters

The type of beaters used has a great deal to do with the quality of sound produced by various drums. It is interesting and worthwhile to experiment with a number of different materials. Here are some suggestions:

Ready-made:

    Empty Bic ball-point pens (point away from the drum)
    Small wooden spoons
    Pieces of $\frac{1}{4}$ in. dowelling, about 10 in. (25 cm) long

Easily made:

    10 in. lengths cut from cane pea sticks, with assorted bindings on the end:

(a) A strip of thin felt, about $\frac{3}{4}$ in. or 2 cm. wide, long enough to build up an effective weight when wrapped several times round the end of the stick.

(b) A similar strip of zinc oxide sticking plaster.

(c) A similar strip of Scotch or PVC adhesive tape.

(d) A wide elastic band, twisted and doubled repeatedly over the end until it is tight.

An advantage of using pea sticks in preference to dowelling is that they are tough and springy. However, for a large drum they will be too light. Further enlargement of the end, without using a thicker stick, will give an unbalanced feeling in the

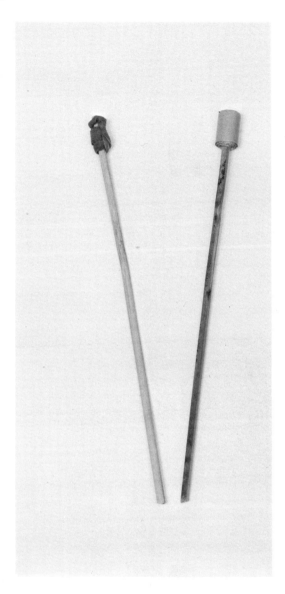

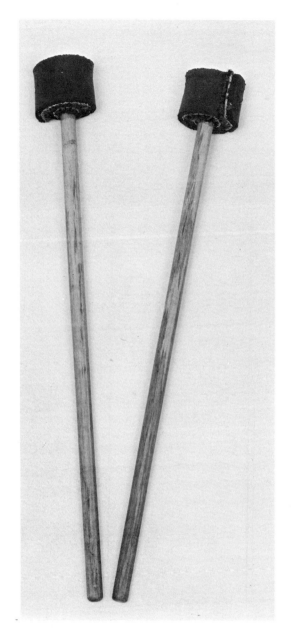

Fig. 11 (*above*) Cane pea-stick beaters, one with an elastic band head, and one with an adhesive tape head; (*right*) timpani sticks made from dowelling and rubber-backed carpet.

hand. Different lengths of stick will also have a different 'feel' about them.

Timpani sticks

For a large drum, a pair of imitation timpani sticks can be made as follows:

Cut two 12 in. lengths of $\frac{3}{8}$ in. dowelling. Bind round the end of each stick a strip of rubber backed carpet, 4 in. by 1 in. (10 cm by 2·5 cm). Use Copydex adhesive like the jam in a swiss roll, and bind the carpet in place until the adhesive has set. This makes a soft-headed stick. For a harder one, build up a core of Sellotape, and cover this with a single layer of carpet, glued on with Copydex. For a harder one still, use felt instead of carpet.

Fig. 12 Playing the 'Talking Drum'—the harder you squeeze,
the higher the note.

3 Kazoos and horns

These are rather surprising instruments—surprising both in their extreme simplicity and in the sounds they can produce. They can be made and played by quite young children.

Most builders' merchants supply rigid plastic cold-water piping in two or three different diameters, ranging from about 1·5 cm to 2·5 cm. These are commonly, if somewhat inaccurately, referred to as 'half-inch' and 'three-quarter inch' sizes. They also supply much larger sizes of a different type, for use as rain water pipes. For our present purpose we are concerned with the sort used for plumbing. This can be easily cut with a miniature hack-saw, and smoothed with a fine file or abrasive paper. It can also be moulded after dipping in hot water.

Horns

These consist of nothing more than pieces of the larger ($\frac{3}{4}$ in.) cold-water piping, with the ends squared and smoothed. They can be anything from 6 in. to 3 ft in length. Their fundamental pitch can be established by tapping one end firmly with the palm of the hand. In fact this is one way of playing them, distributed round a group of players as with handbells. Played as horns, they will each produce their fundamental note with a convincing resonance, after a little practice.

The sound in a brass instrument is produced by blowing steady and controlled 'raspberries' into the mouthpiece, at various pitches which resonate with the harmonic frequencies of the tube. A normal horn mouthpiece has a rim of approximately the same diameter as the piping we are using. The wide parallel bore of the plastic pipe makes production of the higher notes of the harmonic series unsatisfactory and difficult, but the fundamental note will sound quite easily.

The most usual 'embouchure', or lip shape, adopted by horn players, may be described as a 'whistling' or 'puckered' smile. A small elliptical aperture is formed in the centre of the lips where the vibration starts. The note is begun with a 'T' sound.

Instruments played in this way, which include the mediaeval cornetts and serpents, although they were usually made of wood, are called 'lip reed' instruments.

Your first efforts will probably result in a dull spitting noise, out of tune with the speaking pitch of the pipe. With a little practice, aiming to play a steady note at the pitch revealed by tapping the end with the palm of the hand, the sound will come to life. The muscles surrounding the lips will soon learn to provide the correct tension and pressure for various lengths and pitches. 'Pressure' is perhaps misleading—in fact very little will be needed.

A pipe 19$\frac{1}{2}$ in. (49 cm) long will sound the F below middle C. One 16$\frac{1}{2}$ in. (42 cm) long will sound the G next above this. For middle C you will need 12½ in. (32 cm). Doubling the length lowers the pitch by an octave, and vice versa. The best sounds, using ¾ in. piping, lie between the F below middle C and the C an octave above it. Longer pipes need a larger bore for their fundamental note to speak clearly, although they will sound their second harmonic, an octave-and-a-fifth above the fundamental, quite well.

Various experiments can prove interesting. For instance, you could try the effect of holding the end of the pipe inside an empty jar or box, while sounding the note. You might also try making one or two large finger holes, starting a few inches from the end, to play different notes. (There are six in a mediaeval cornett, but its bore is conical, and its dimensions exact; and this number will not work in a cylindrical pipe.) Three or four pipes, playing the notes of a chord or a scale, can be bound together side by side, with small spacing pieces between them, to make a kind of giant mouth organ.

Horn chords

The most effective way of using these straight horns is in groups of three or more players, sounding the notes of the primary triads in harmony. Many traditional and other tunes can then be harmonized.

The notes of the primary triads, in several different keys, are set out in Chapter 5, p. 53. Played on these horns, perhaps with some guitars and chime-bars to help, and voices or recorders improvising a melody above them, the effect can be unique and surprising.

Kazoo

Most boys and girls have tried, at some time or other, humming through a piece of tissue paper held against a comb. Cheap toy instruments often incorporate a similar device, and disappointment sometimes results from not realizing that they have to be hummed through, not merely blown. Put technically, they use a membrane, or thin diaphragm, to cause acoustical reinforcement and distortion of the voice.

To make a rather superior kind of kazoo, cut off about 5 in. (13 cm) of the narrower (half inch) cold water piping. Dip one end in boiling water for a few seconds, and squeeze the opposite sides of the tube together, with a gloved hand, or by pressing down with a flat piece of wood. This should leave a flattened slit as a mouthpiece, like the end of a motor cycle exhaust pipe, about ⅛ in. wide.

Cut a 'V'-shaped window, ¾ in. (2 cm) long, as shown in Fig. 13(a), using a miniature hack-saw. Smooth the edges with glass-paper. With a little contact adhesive, glue over this window a piece of the thinnest plastic tissue you can find. Cooked meat or bacon is often wrapped in it. The thinner it is, the better your kazoo will work. Ordinary tissue paper is quite satisfactory, but will not last so long.

Cut off another piece of piping, 1⅛ in. (3 cm) long. If possible, use a contrasting colour. Slit it longways, so that it can be opened out to fit over the window of the kazoo. Punch the centres for a pattern of holes, as shown in Fig. 13 (c), and drill them with a 5/32 in. drill, cleaning off any remaining burr. Dip the plastic in boiling water for a very short time, holding it with a pair of pliers or tongs, and open the slit out to about ¼ in. Put a little more

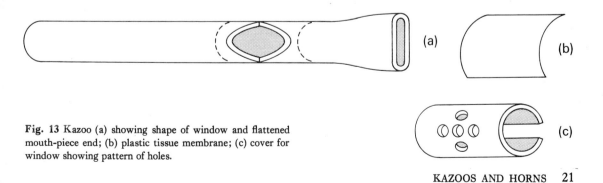

Fig. 13 Kazoo (a) showing shape of window and flattened mouth-piece end; (b) plastic tissue membrane; (c) cover for window showing pattern of holes.

Fig. 14 (*above*) Kazoo horn; (*below*) Kazoo.

contact adhesive on the kazoo, level with the window, and ask a friend to hold it while you spring the cover open, just enough to slide it into position without damaging the tissue. The kazoo is now ready.

Kazoo-horn

This somewhat startling device, while not exactly sweet-toned, provides an interesting example of still more acoustical reinforcement.

Simply take one of the straight horns, and add a kazoo window, with tissue and a cover, near the top. Play it as a horn, but not too late at night, especially if you can manage the second harmonic.

4 Flutes

These fascinating instruments have existed, in various forms, since Stone Age times. The earliest known specimens were made by boring through the leg bones of animals, and in the later Stone Age, clay was used. A rock drawing of this period shows a flute being played by a dancer wearing a diabolical-looking mask and animal skin. In the ritualistic function of all ancient instruments, the flute seems to have been associated with fertility rites.

Broadly speaking, a flute is an instrument in which the sound is generated by a stream of air striking a sharp edge, and thereby setting up vibrations in the column of air inside a tube. There are three principle ways of achieving this: by blowing with pursed lips across the mouth of a narrow tube; by similarly blowing across a hole in the side of a tube which is closed at one end; and by using a whistle or 'fipple'.

In the first, the tube is normally stopped, or plugged at one end. The pitch of the note depends partly on the extent to which the player's mouth covers the open end, and partly on the length of the tube. A tuned set of these pipes, usually seven or nine in number, and bound together like a raft, or placed in a case, is called a Syrinx, or pan-pipes. Versions of this instrument have appeared, and are still in use, in parts of central Europe, the Solomon Islands, and in China, where it is known as the 'Lu'. Traditionally it is the instrument of shepherds and herdsmen, not easy to play, but very effective in capable hands.

In the second, where the blowing hole is in the side of the tube near the stopped end, the sounding length is varied by opening and closing finger-holes, with the instrument held sideways. Here we have the transverse flute, the basis of the modern orchestral instrument.

In the third way, by a device known for thousands of years, the pursed lips of the player are replaced by a block in the top of the pipe, leaving a narrow channel through which the air is directed on to a sharp edge or 'lip'. The old English name for the block is 'fipple'. Instruments which use this include flageolets, recorders and pipe organs. They have the advantage of sure success when blown, but remove from the player most of the possibilities of lip-controlled expression.

Flutes you can make

Throughout the ages a variety of materials have been used in making these instruments, including bone, clay, bamboo, boxwood, ivory, rosewood, ebony, glass, silver, and in recent times, plastics.

For the pan-pipes and the transverse flutes described in this chapter you will need some of the plastic cold water piping mentioned in Chapter 2 for making horns and kazoos.

Pan-pipes

Before making a set of these, you could find out whether you have an aptitude for playing a rim-blown instrument, by blowing across the top of a small tonic water or similar bottle. Place the rim just under the lower lip, and purse the lips as if smiling a little. Aim to direct a gentle stream of air on to the opposite side of the rim. Experiment with the angle of the bottle, and the relative position of the upper and lower lips. With some practice, a clear note should result. A set of these bottles may be tuned to play a scale by pouring in water to the correct levels.

Materials

To make a nine-note instrument, with the F next above middle C as its lowest note, you will need the following:

2 metres of Marley 16 mm UPVC overflow piping (approximate internal diameter 12 mm; wall thickness 2 mm) or equivalent size in any other make.
One piece of 6 mm plywood, 30 cm by 15 cm (12 in. by 6 in.)
David's Isopon, of Holt's Cataloy paste filler and hardener (small size pack, as stocked by most car accessory shops)
Some thin twine for binding.

Tools

Miniature hack-saw; small round and flat files; fret-saw or coping saw; abrasive paper; bench hook.

The pipes

These are the lengths of piping needed for the various notes:

F or **F sharp** 25·3 cm; **G** 22·4 cm; **A** 20·2 cm; **B** or **B flat** 18·4 cm; **C′** 17 cm; **D′** 15 cm; **E′** 13·7 cm; **F′** or **F sharp′** 12·8 cm; **G** 11·5 cm.

To make a square cut in a piece of plastic piping, first mark the position by wrapping a piece of adhesive tape carefully round, with one edge at the cutting place. Saw gently, rotating the pipe in the angle of a bench hook as you go. Remove the tape, and smooth off all the burr with fine abrasive

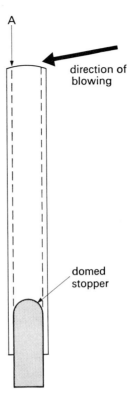

Fig. 15 Pan-pipes, sectional view of pipe with stopper.

paper, which can be rolled round a pencil for the inside of the pipe.

Shape the top ends of the pipes as shown in Fig. 15, using a fine file, and being careful to leave a clean, sharp edge at A.

Stoppers

From the remainder of the piping, cut nine pieces each 4 cm long, and smooth the ends. Mix about enough polyester paste and hardener to fill three of these at a time. (It hardens fairly quickly.) Push the paste in from one end with a small flat piece of wood, until it extrudes from the other end. Do not push it in from both ends as this will trap air in the middle. Heat is generated during the 'curing' process, and the material will have hardened by the time it has cooled down again. When ready, a sharp tap on the end should free the stoppers from their moulds, after which they can be pushed out with a piece of dowelling. They should come out very cleanly.

Square the ends of the stoppers, reducing their length to 3·5 cm, and form the tops to a dome shape, as shown in Fig. 15, using a file and abrasive paper. This shape results in a clearer note than if a flat-topped stopper is used.

Push the stoppers into their pipes until there is exactly 15 mm still showing. This should produce a scale of F major. The B flat can be tuned to B natural by pushing its stopper in a further 6 mm, giving a scale of C major. If the low F stopper is then pushed in another 12 mm, and the upper F 6 mm, both the F's will have become F sharps, and the scale will now be that of G major. To flatten a note, pull the stopper out a little way.

At this stage it is a good idea to write the letter names of the notes on the ends of the stoppers for reference, and to test each one for air-tightness by blowing through the top of the pipe. Even a very slight leak will prevent the note from speaking properly. If necessary, a little vaseline smeared on the stopper should cure this. Minute variations occur very occasionally on the internal diameter of the piping, and a loose stopper can be the result of using too narrow a mould.

Ease of tone production also depends on the exact shape and sharpness of the rim of the pipe. If some notes seem to sound better than others, it is worth trying to discover the reason.

The frame

The design shown in Fig. 16 provides convenient handles, and has an attractive appearance, resembling the wings of a bird. Handles are not essential, however, and a simple strip of wood will do. For the wing-shaped frame, the shape is drawn on the piece of plywood, and cut out with a fretsaw or coping saw. The edges should be smoothed carefully before the wood is painted or varnished.

When the frame is ready, lay the pipes in position, and mark on the wood where their centres will come, leaving just enough space between each one for the binding twine to pass through. Wrap some coarse abrasive paper round a piece of $\frac{1}{2}$ in. dowelling, and with this make a shallow trough to

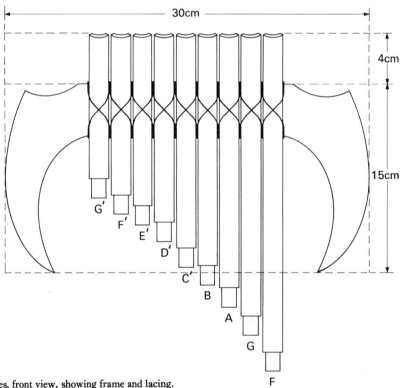

Fig. 16 Pan-pipes, front view, showing frame and lacing.

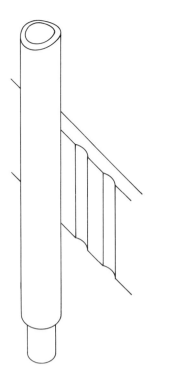

Fig. 17 Pan-pipes—troughs shaped in wooden frame to locate pipes.

receive each pipe, at right-angles to the top of the frame, to ensure correct alignment. Glue the pipes in position with epoxy or contact adhesive, making sure that all the tops are level, and facing the same way.

Binding is a matter for individual inventiveness. One way is to loop the twine behind the wood, and form a cross over each pipe, finally tying the ends together and glueing them to the underneath of the wood. With white or coloured twine, and the wood painted to contrast with the pipes, this will be quite a handsome-looking instrument. Some practice is needed to play it, and you may get dizzy from too much blowing until the necessary skill has been gained to produce the maximum effect with the minimum amount of breath.

Transverse flutes

The typical 'Renaissance' or German flute was a side-blown instrument made from a plain cylindrical tube of boxwood, with six finger holes. It was a deeper and more mellow-toned descendant of the ancient and shrill flutes which had come to

Europe from the East in the Middle Ages, and was common in three sizes: treble, tenor and bass. It was not easy to play in tune, since the finger holes were spaced as much for the convenience of the player as for accuracy of pitch. It had considerable charm, but was not popular in the orchestras of the 17th Century. The flute parts written by Purcell, Handel and others were intended for recorders, whose cross-fingering enabled them to play well in tune in any key, and with some agility. Expressive playing on recorders depended on tonguing and phrasing, rather than on dynamic range, and this was in accord with the musical tastes of the time. In the 18th Century, however, the transverse flute was given a conical bore, separate joints for tuning, and a few semitone keys, and in its new form, not long before the dawn of the 'Romantic' era, it ousted the recorder almost entirely, achieving immense popularity both as an orchestral and as a domestic amateur and solo instrument.

Cylindrical flute

This is a simple instrument for a beginner to make. Afterwards it can be modified in several ways which will greatly improve its tone and range.

Materials

These materials will be sufficient to make a treble flute in F, which is a convenient pitch for playing along with recorders, and also enables the finger holes to be large enough to produce a good tone, while still within the player's reach:

A piece of plastic cold water piping, 60 cm (2 ft) long, with an internal diameter as near as possible to 17 mm, and a wall thickness of about 2 mm. (This is a standard size, but the material varies a little from one make to another.)

A small quantity of David's Isopon Paste or Cataloy Paste and hardener.

A piece of 4 mm or 6 mm plywood, at least 50 cm by 4 cm (20 in. by $1\frac{3}{4}$ in.).

A strip of wood about 2 cm by 1·5 cm, or $\frac{1}{2}$ in. by $\frac{3}{4}$ in., at least 50 cm long.

Tools

A bench with a vice, or a bench hook with an assistant.

Miniature hack-saw.

Two small 'G' cramps, or some strong string, or P.V.C. adhesive tape.

A hand-drill with a chuck large enough to take drills up to $\frac{3}{8}$ in. diameter, with the following drill sizes: $\frac{5}{32}$ in.; $\frac{1}{4}$ in.; $\frac{5}{16}$ in.; $\frac{3}{8}$ in.; and a countersink bit or handled countersink.

Small fine files, flat and round.

Fine abrasive paper.

The body of the flute

Cut off exactly 49·2 cm of the piping, with carefully squared ends. Clean and smooth the ends, inside and out.

Jig for drilling the holes

Reduce the length of the piece of plywood to exactly 49·2 cm, and mark on it accurately the positions for the holes, using the measurements given in Fig. 19. Glue and panel-pin the strip of wood to its underside, with the inner edge of the strip 11 mm from, and parallel to, the line of the hole centres. This makes in effect a wooden girder, into the angle of which the pipe will be clamped for drilling.

Prick the exact centres of the holes in the piece of plywood with a large nail, or other sharp-pointed implement, and drill them to $\frac{5}{32}$ in. It is now a simple matter to clamp or bind the pipe in position, with its ends just level with the ends of the jig, and drill all the holes to $\frac{5}{32}$ in. including the embouchure or blowing hole. Keep the drill perpendicular to the flute, and do not attempt to make the holes without using a jig, as the drill would then almost certainly wander away from its intended positions, and the pipe would be wasted.

Before enlarging the holes to their correct sizes, remove the flute from the jig, which can be used again any number of times. Note the sizes carefully, and check that you have the flute the way round you think you have. The finger hole nearest to the end should be $\frac{1}{4}$ in. in diameter, and all the other finger holes, $\frac{5}{16}$ in. The embouchure hole can be drilled to $\frac{3}{8}$ in.

Fig. 18 Playing the pan-pipes.

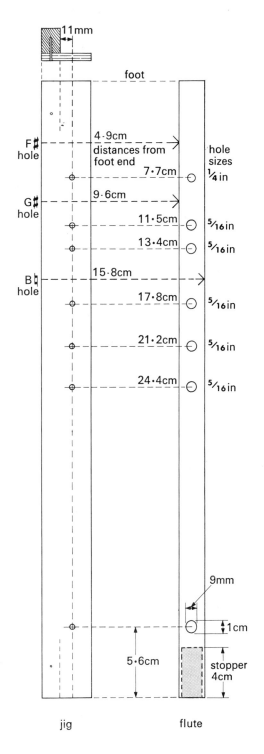

Fig. 19 Plan of flute and jig showing scale measurements. All the holes in the jig are $\frac{5}{32}$ in.

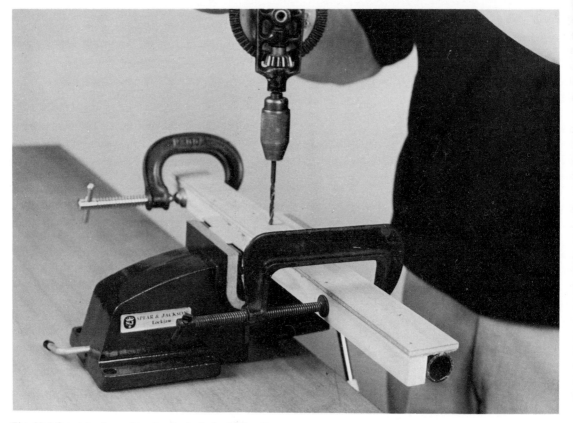

Fig. 20 A flute tube clamped in place in the jig for drilling the sound holes.

It is important to clean off all traces of burr from the insides of the pipe and the holes, with a fine round file, and a screw of abrasive paper. The tops of the finger holes (*not* the embouchure hole) may be very slightly chamfered with a countersink bit held in the hand.

The embouchure hole

Again using a fine round file, enlarge the embouchure hole a little, lengthwise only, to an elliptical shape, and make it at the same time slightly conical, opening out into the flute as shown in Fig.

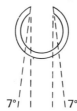

Fig. 21 Section at embouchure hole.　　7°| | | |7°

21. It is essential to have a clean, sharp edge all round the top of this hole. Very fine abrasive paper, wrapped round a pencil, will give a good finish. The final size, which affects the tuning and tone of the instrument, should be 9 mm across and 10 mm longways, at the outer surface.

The stopper

This is usually referred to as the 'cork'. Its length and fit are very important. A poorly fitting piece of cork or dowelling will not really work. It is far more satisfactory to use polyester filler, moulded to the exact size, as described for the pan-pipes on p. 25. A piece of piping 5 cm long, cut from the same piping as the flute, should be used as a mould. When the plastic has hardened, its length is reduced accurately to 4 cm, with the ends squared and smoothed. It should be a fairly tight fit in the end of the flute. If it slides about too easily, secure and seal it with a very small amount of contact adhesive; not enough to prevent it from being pushed out again if necessary. When the stopper is in its correct position, exactly level with the end of the tube near the embouchure hole, the flute, in its simplest form, is ready.

At this point, unless you already know how to play a flute, you may begin to think you have made one which is no good. Do not worry; this is quite normal at first, and it would be the same if you had bought an expensive professional instrument.

The flute should be held like a recorder, with the left hand nearer the mouth than the right, and then pointed towards the player's right hand side. It is better not actually to cover any of the holes until you can produce a sound. Practice pursing the moistened lips, in a half-smiling fashion, aiming to direct a flattened stream of air gently across the mouth hole. Roll the instrument slightly in either direction, and experiment with the relative positions of the upper and lower lip, until a clear note begins to come. Try to articulate each note with a 'T' sound, withdrawing the tongue again immediately. It may take several days, but once the knack is acquired, it will soon develop.

With all the holes uncovered, you should be sounding the note E. (See fingering chart on p. 39.) Next try adding the first finger of the left hand, then the second, and so on, until eventually the lowest note, the F next above middle C on the piano, can be sounded. The higher octave is produced by 'overblowing', that is, by slightly compressing the lips and blowing a little harder.

Simple tunes for beginners on the treble recorder will provide useful practice, as soon as you can begin to sound some clear notes.

Modifications

If your basic flute was accurately made, you can improve its performance very considerably by applying to it some of the acoustical principles discovered by Theobald Boehm.

Boehm (1794–1881) was a jeweller and a scientist, as well as being a distinguished German flautist. Much impressed by the tone resulting from the unusually large finger holes of a particular English player's instrument, he undertook extensive researches into the acoustics of flutes. After years of experimenting, he virtually invented the modern orchestral flute, with its ingenious key-work, enabling the player to operate large and otherwise inaccessible tone holes, and to play with agility, accuracy and power in any key. The following significant passage is translated from his own treatise:

'The formation of the nodes and segments of the sound waves takes place most easily and perfectly in a cylindrical flute tube, the length of which is thirty times its diameter, and in which a contraction begins in the upper fourth part of the length of the tube, continuing to the cork, where the diameter is reduced to nine-tenths.'

This refers to Boehm's use of the so-called 'parabolic head', a reversal of the 18th Century practice of tapering the bore from the head joint towards the foot. Boehm also specified that the thickness of the material at the mouth hole should be 4 mm, and that the cork should be at a distance from the centre of the mouth hole exactly equal to the diameter at that point, if the octaves were to sound in tune. He recommended that the sides of the embouchure hole should slope away at an angle of not more than 7°, and that the inside of the flute should be perfectly smooth, to eliminate hissing noises.

We cannot convert our cylindrical plastic flute into a perfect specimen according to Boehm's recommendations, but we can go quite a long way towards this. All, or any, of the following modifications will be beneficial in some way.

Parabolic head

From a piece of $\frac{3}{4}$ in. dowelling, saw a thin tapering wedge, 10 cm long, and 3 mm thick at its widest

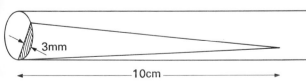

3mm

10cm

Fig. 22 Cutting the wedge for the parabolic head.

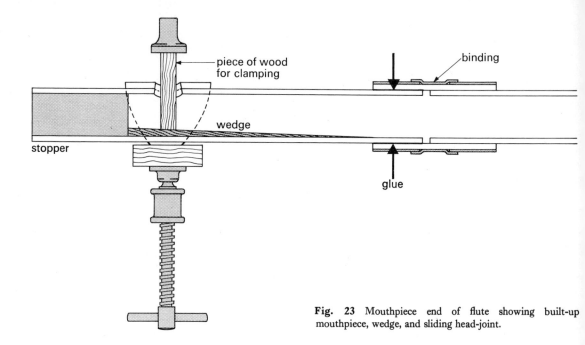

Fig. 23 Mouthpiece end of flute showing built-up mouthpiece, wedge, and sliding head-joint.

part, as illustrated in Fig. 22. The flat side should be filed and sanded as smooth as possible. Apply two or three coats of polyurethane varnish to prevent the wood from becoming clogged with moisture. Remove the stopper from the flute, by pushing it out from the far end with a long rod. Ensure that all is dry, and glue the wedge to the inside of the bottom of the tube, opposite the embouchure hole, using either an epoxy, or a waterproof contact, adhesive. Refit the stopper and use it to push the wedge into its correct position. The widest part should rest against the stopper. To secure the wedge in place while the glue sets, insert a small piece of wood through the embouchure hole, and press it gently in a vice, or with a clamp.

When the flute is ready again, there should be a noticeable increase in clarity and power through the whole of its compass.

Built-up mouthpiece

This will enhance the appearance, as well as having a further considerable effect on the tone production. It can be made from a piece of the same piping as the flute tube, although a contrasting colour looks better. Whatever tubing is used, it should have the same internal diameter as

the flute, or slightly more.

By sawing obliquely, cut out a 'V'-shaped piece which is 3·5 cm long at the top, and 1·5 cm at the bottom, as illustrated in Fig. 25. Make a saw cut through the narrowest part, parallel with the bore. Smooth and slightly round off all the edges. Drill a small ($\frac{5}{32}$ in.) pilot hole in the centre of the widest part, opposite the saw cut, and enlarge the hole to $\frac{3}{8}$ in. Immerse the plastic in boiling water for a few seconds to soften it, open it out a little, and slide it on to the flute so that the new hole coincides with the existing embouchure hole. While the plastic is still warm, squeeze it tightly all round, so as to mould it to a good fit.

Remove it again, and place a little fast-setting epoxy adhesive all round the embouchure hole. Spring the new mouthpiece open sufficiently to slide it on clear of the glue, and position it exactly. Loop some elastic bands tightly around it until the glue has set. The new embouchure hole can then be formed to its correct elliptical and conical shape as before, with the same external measurements, using a fine round file, followed by very fine abrasive paper. If the hole has clean, sharp edges and smooth sides, the improvement in tone production should be very obvious.

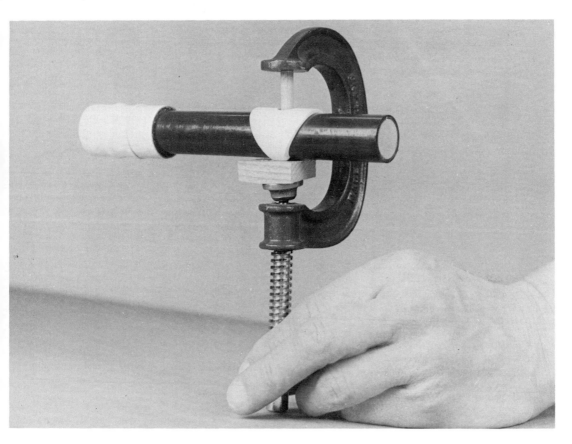

Fig. 24 Head joint of flute—using a short piece of dowelling to clamp the wedge in place while the glue sets.

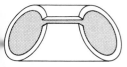

Fig. 25 Plastic sleeve for built-up mouthpiece.

Sliding head joint

As with the previous modification, this will improve both the appearance and the functioning of the instrument. It will facilitate tuning, cleaning and stowage.

All wind instruments rise in pitch as they become warmer, and players compensate for this by slightly pulling out the joints, so as to lengthen the vibrating column of air. Ideally, the finger holes should then be spaced out proportionally, but in practice this would be an unnecessary complication, since the intonation on all breath-blown instruments is controlled to some extent by the player's diaphragm and mouth.

To make the sliding joint, you will need the following additional materials:

A short piece of plastic waste pipe, large enough in diameter to fit loosely round the flute (Bartol Waste Systems, $1\frac{1}{4}$ in., or any equivalent, from a builders' merchant).

Some thin but strong adhesive tape, which will stretch a little (good quality PVC adhesive tape, 19 mm width ($\frac{3}{4}$ in.) is the most suitable).

Cut off 5 cm of the waste pipe. If it is of the tough and fibrous type it may be trimmed with a

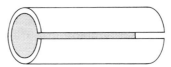

Fig. 26 Plastic sleeve for sliding head-joint.

chisel or a sharp knife. Make a straight saw cut in it, parallel to its length. Soften the plastic in boiling water for a short time, and wrap it tightly round the flute to form a sleeve. Mark with a knife, at both ends of the sleeve, where the overlap begins, and carefully cut away the spare material. Trim the edges until they only just meet when the sleeve is wrapped really closely round the flute; otherwise it will leak.

The next operation is perhaps best carried out at dead of night, when nobody else is about. Your friends may have thought you were a little mad to be making a flute from plastic water pipe. They will surely now be confirmed in their view if they see you sawing the instrument in two, 16 cm from the stopped end.

The mouthpiece end will be referred to from now on as the head joint, and the other part as the foot joint. Remove about 3 mm from the foot joint, where it will butt against the head, to enable the flute to be tuned to the slightly higher pitch of many new Japanese and Continental instruments. The ends should be squared and cleaned.

Fig. 27 Putting the centre binding on to the sleeve of the sliding head-joint.

Spread some waterproof contact adhesive thinly and evenly round the outside of the head joint for a distance of 15 mm from the sleeve end. Place the sleeve on this section with an overlap of 2 cm, and with the cut on the underside. Bind it tightly round, four times, with some white PVC tape, at this point, keeping the tape exactly level with the end of the sleeve, and finishing at the bottom. Now insert the foot joint, (but do not glue it) and bind that end of the sleeve in the same way, ensuring that the cut in the bottom is closed up. It is essential to have a really close fit all round. Finally, bind the centre with a third piece of tape, still going round four times, stretching the tape a little way over the two end bindings, and filling the central gap. If this is done neatly with white PVC tape, it will look almost like a piece of turned ivory. If the ends of the tape persist in coming away, a touch of contact adhesive will secure them. To make the sleeve completely airtight, smear a little vaseline on the joint.

Semitone keys

The key described here can be fitted in any or all of three positions on the treble flute in F, to play F

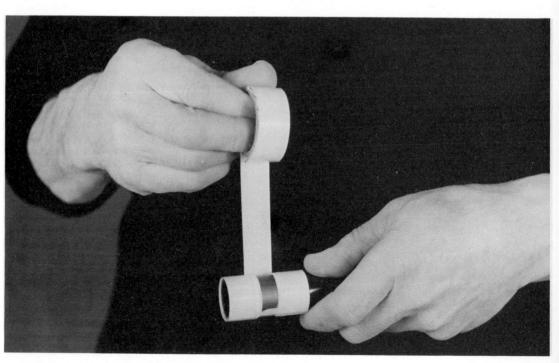

sharp, G sharp or B natural. With more than three keys, the instrument becomes rather cumbersome. In any case, C sharp and E flat can be cross-fingered, as shown in the fingering chart on p. 39.

The lever is made from a piece of close-grained hardwood such as beech, sycamore, boxwood or ramin, or it can be a piece of 6 mm birch plywood. It can be varnished, or painted white. The exact shape of the key in relation to the height of its pivot is important, if it is not to leak, and thereby prevent any of the notes below it from sounding.

Draw the shape carefully on the wood as shown (see Fig. 28), with the grain of the wood parallel to the thinner end, and the position of the hole pricked. Drill the hole exactly at right-angles to the wood, with a $\frac{1}{16}$ in. drill, and cut out the key with a fret-saw, or other fine saw.

The pad is backed by a 12 mm square cut from plastic pipe of the same diameter as the flute. To attach this to the lever, an $\frac{1}{8}$ in. hole is drilled in the centre of the plastic square, and continued a short way into the underside of the thicker end of the key, as shown in the diagram. The plastic is then glued in place, using Araldite Rapid or a fast-setting equivalent. The holes should be lined up exactly, and an extra drop of glue allowed to fill them both, overflowing just enough to form a 'rivet head' in the centre of the plastic. If the key is held upside down and level in a vice while the glue

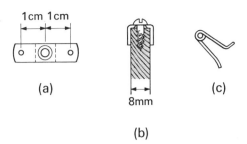

Fig. 29 (a) Bracket before bending; (b) bending the bracket; (c) the spring.

hardens, no further pressure or clamping will be needed. It will be seen from Fig. 28 that the curvature of the plastic square follows that of the key.

The bracket

Mark a strip, 25 mm by 7 mm, on a piece of thin and preferably rustless metal, such as an old aluminium saucepan, or the spreader from a tin of contact adhesive. Tin cans are too thin, but the metal must be malleable enough to bend fairly easily without breaking. Punch accurately the positions for the three holes, as shown. Drill the two smaller ones $\frac{1}{16}$ in., and the centre one $\frac{5}{32}$ in., countersunk, to take a No 4 BA countersunk screw.

Cut out the strip, with the ends slightly rounded. The two lugs should now be bent at right-angles. The best way to achieve this is to screw the strip through its centre hole, with the countersink the wrong way round, to the edge of a piece of wood 8 mm thick, and squeeze the two ends tightly round the corners with a pair of pliers. If any further bending is needed, support the base of the bracket with a pair of thin-nosed pliers, so that the metal surrounding the centre hole does not bend.

Drill an $\frac{1}{8}$ in. hole in the flute, in line with the finger holes; 4·9 cm from the foot end. (Punch a place for the hole first, or the drill may slip.) Screw the bracket to the flute with a No. 4 BA countersunk screw, shortened so that it only just protrudes inside the flute. A very small taper, filed on the end of the screw, will help it to enter the hole and form a thread in the plastic. Secure the bracket with the pivot holes parallel to the length of the flute, but be careful not to over-tighten the screw. A touch of glue under the bracket will help.

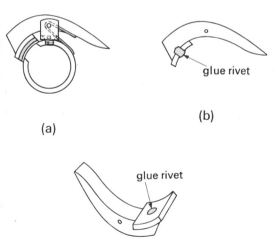

Fig. 28 Flute key; (a) sectional view of flute showing key; (b) side view of key; (*below*) underneath view of key with plastic square and glue rivet.

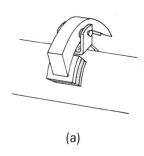

(a)

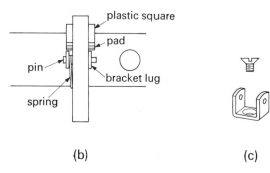

plastic square

pad

pin

bracket lug

spring

(b)   (c)

Fig. 30 (a) and (b) The key in position on the flute shown from two angles and (c) the mounting bracket and 4BA countersunk screw

Sound hole for F sharp key

This is drilled to $\frac{1}{4}$ in. diameter, with its centre 4·9 cm from the foot end, and 1 cm round the circumference from the screw hole, on the side away from the player's right hand. Remove all traces of burr from the edges of the hole.

The spring

Use the smallest size of safety-pin, about $\frac{3}{4}$ in. long. Cut off the head, and bend the point as shown in Fig. 29(c).

The pivot pin

Select a panel pin just thick enough to fit fairly tightly through the holes in the lugs and the key, and shorten it so that about 2 mm will eventually protrude. File the end to a blunt point.

The pad

On this the success of the key will largely depend. It can be made from a 12 mm square of thin felt, covered with a similar sized piece cut from a cycle puncture repair patch.

It is important not to glue the pad in place until the rest of the key has been mounted and sprung.

Fig. 31 Flute keys: notice their position relative to the finger holes.

Assembly

Push the pivot pin into one lug of the bracket. Place the eye of the spring on the end of the pin, between the lugs, with the bent point uppermost. It may be necessary to thin the centre of the key lever until it just fits into the remaining space, but it should not wobble. Continue to push the pin through the hole in the key, and on, until it emerges from the other lug of the bracket. If it is too stiff to push in, support the bracket on the narrowly opened jaws of a vice, and gently tap the head of the pin with a light hammer, allowing the end of the pin to pass between the jaws. Press the angled point of the spring down under the finger end of the key, and slide the other end of the spring along under the key, so that it stays in place.

Next put some Copydex adhesive on each side of the felt square, and place the pad, with its rubber face, in position. Allow the spring pressure to clamp it, and leave it to set. Dust a little talcum powder on the face of the pad, and the key should then work. If it does, the lowest note will speak as clearly and easily as before. If not, there are several things to check.

The first thing to do is to try playing the flute the wrong way round, with the hands reversed, which will enable you to press the pad of the key with the left little finger. If this cures the trouble, a leaky pad is indicated. Remove the spring, open it out a little, replace it, and try again. If the leak persists, place a further square of puncture repair rubber between the pad and the flute. If this works, glue it in place and be thankful. (Remember to glue it on one side only.)

If there is still a leak, there must be some fault in the construction of the key. Check that the pad lies centrally over the sound hole, and parallel to it

line of finger holes

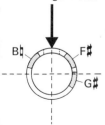

Fig. 32 Positions of sound holes for keys shown from foot end.

when closed. If not, it may be because you have drilled a hole in the wrong place, or at the wrong angle. For this there are two possible remedies. One is to begin again, and the other is to abandon the enterprise altogether, and settle for an unkeyed flute, in which case a piece of white PVC tape wrapped around the tube will cover the two unwanted holes in a reasonably decorative manner.

B natural

If the F sharp key is a success, a similar one, facing the opposite way round, can be fitted between the B flat and C holes for the note B natural. For this the sound hole should be 15·8 cm from the foot end of the flute, $\frac{1}{4}$ in. in diameter, and 1 cm round the circumference from the screw hole, on the side away from the player's left hand.

G sharp

There is also room for a G sharp key, facing the same way round as the one for F sharp, between G and A. The sound hole for G sharp should be 1 cm further round the flute than the F sharp hole, likewise $\frac{1}{4}$ in. in diameter, and 9·6 cm from the foot end.

With these three keys, it is possible to play a fully chromatic scale up as far as C in the second octave. The cross-fingerings suggested in the fingering chart for C sharp and E flat do not overblow by an octave, and therefore cannot be used in the upper register, but the upper D, E and F will sound, and upper E flat is possible with the different fingering shown.

Alternative pitches

On the unkeyed flute in F, there is no satisfactory system of cross-fingering to produce the notes F sharp, G sharp, or B natural, in tune and with a good tone. Holes for the little fingers could be reached, but they would make the flute much more difficult to play. It is possible to make foot joints of different lengths for use with the same head. For example, a foot joint 26·5 cm long, on the flute we have made, will sound treble clef G as its lowest note, and one 37·5 cm long will go down to the E flat below that. Beyond these limits, the diameter of the tube would be too far from the prescribed fraction of its length to work efficiently, and piping

Fig. 33 Playing the transverse flute.

of a larger diameter would be needed.

For flutes of different pitches, the spacing and size of the finger holes has to be scaled up or down in proportion to the total sounding length of the tube; that is, from the centre of the embouchure hole to the far end of the foot joint. An economical way to experiment with the size and spacing of the holes is to cover any unsuccessful ones with adhesive tape, until there is no room left to make any more holes. When drilling in the plastic without using a jig, always prick the centre of the

hole first, to prevent the drill from slipping suddenly.

A piccolo flute, or fife, pitched in high C or E flat, can be made from the same sized tubing a the pan-pipes, described on p. 25. The largest size of vent or overflow piping normally available, with an internal diameter of about 19 mm, is big enough for a tenor flute, with middle C or B flat as its lowest note. Unfortunately, if the finger holes are to be of sufficient size to produce a good tone, this instrument can only be played by a person with exceptionally large hands. This was one of the

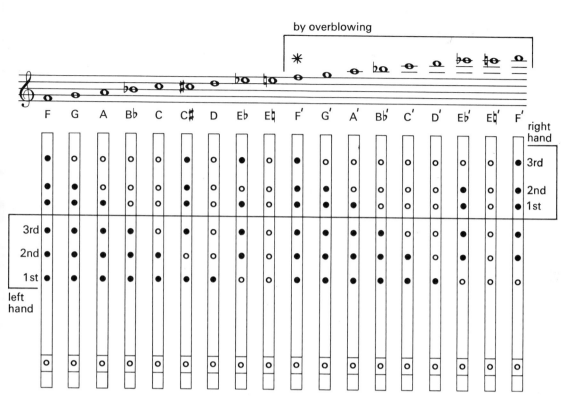

Fig. 34 Fingering chart for a six-holed unkeyed treble flute in F. * This note can also be played by slightly rolling the left fore-finger.

problems which Boehm set out to solve. His solution requires technology beyond the means of the amateur. However, readers with an inventive turn of mind might, after studying the preceding section on semitone keys, be able to devise a system of finger plates to cover inaccessible holes, perhaps using small hinges as pivots.

5 Coke-hod dulcimers

Besides having possibilities as a drum (see Chapter 2), the humble coke-hod forms a useful resonator for this stringed instrument, which may fairly be described as a dulcimer in that it can produce chordal effects when played with wooden beaters. It is also a kind of harp; but then it can be played with one, or even two violin bows, so perhaps it needs a new name altogether. Meanwhile, 'dulcimer' is convenient.

This is the kind of instrument which has an immediate appeal to children, or to folk music groups. A beginner can soon learn to use it for three-chord accompaniments, and it provides quite a resonant bass. It is not difficult to make, and it stands in tune better than a guitar, since the string tension on one side is balanced by that on the other. It may be fitted to various kinds of resonating box, but a plastic coke-hod, if one can be found, is particularly suitable, giving the instrument a slim and attractive appearance, and being easily portable. However, since the coke-hod now seems to be fast disappearing in this age of oil and gas-fired central heating, the making of a box, similar in shape, is described later in the chapter.

Nine steel guitar strings are spaced in the form of a horse-shoe, around a central strut, and tuned so that playing on one side or the other will produce chords, and on alternate sides, scales or tunes.

To make the dulcimer you will need:

Strut

A piece of what used to be known as 'two-by-one batten' (5 cm by 2·5 cm or thereabouts), 3 ft 4 in. (1 metre) long, preferably of beech, mahogany, oak or ramin, but ordinary soft pine will do if the knots are small and infrequent. The dulcimer in the photograph has a scroll on the top made from an old clock spring. A piece of aluminium, duralumin, or moulded perspex could be used instead.

Strings

Medium gauge steel guitar strings (cheapest quality): three No. 2 (B); three No. 3 (G); three No. 4 (D). Alternatively, the instrument can be strung using three No. 1(E); three No. 2(B); and three No. 3(G); requiring less tension, and producing a more 'Oriental' quality of sound.

Bridges

Eighteen wood screws, 1 in. size 6, brass or chromium, with round or raised heads.

Hitch-pins (for anchoring the lower ends of the strings)

Nine 1 in. wire nails.

Wrest-pins (tuning pins)

Nine No. 2 BA nuts and bolts, 1 in. long, with slotted heads; preferably brass, but steel will do.

Fine-tuners

Nine 1 in. by $\frac{3}{16}$ in. Whitworth-threaded steel bolts with wing nuts and washers. Most hardware or Do-it-Yourself shops sell these nuts, bolts and washers in pre-packaged quantities. Some still stock them loose.

Metalwork

In making the dulcimer, and also the psalteries in Chapter 6, a certain amount of hack-sawing, drilling and filing of metal has to be done, and for this a small metalworking vice is a great asset. When holding a screw, the thread will be saved from damage if a small piece of scrap wood is placed on either side of it. The vice may then be screwed up tightly.

The strut

Square the bottom end of the strut, and saw the top to an angle of about 25°, as shown in the diagram. The overall length should still be 1 metre.

Lay the strut on one side, noting which way round it is in relation to the sloping top, and mark out accurately the positions for the pins, screws and bolts at either end, according to the measurements given in Fig. 36. This is best done with a carpenter's square and marking gauge, but a ruler and set square will do almost as well. Prick the exact positions of the holes with a sharp-pointed implement, to ensure accurate drilling.

Repeat this process on the other side of the strut, being sure to look at the right part of the diagram, as the arrangement of the strings is not the same on each side.

Finally, mark and prick the longer of the two narrow sides, for the bass (C) string.

Varnishing

This is a good point at which to smooth the strut, and varnish it with three of four coats of clear polyurethane varnish.

A careful study of the diagram (Fig. 37(a)) will show how the strings are arranged in their three different gauges. The one for each successively higher note is shorter by 8 cm than the preceding one of the same gauge. This enables the tension to

Fig. 35 Coke-hod dulcimer, with clock-spring scroll.

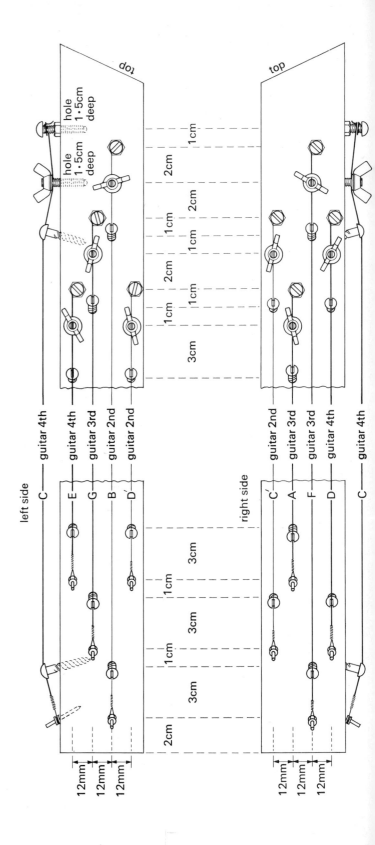

Fig. 36 Top and bottom ends of strut showing stringing layout and spacing of strings. String lengths between bridge screws: C, F, B—82 cm; D, G, C—74 cm; E, A, D¹—66 cm.

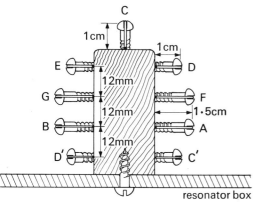

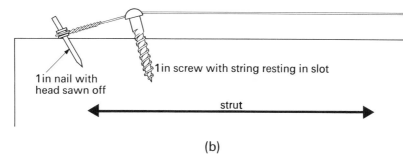

Fig. 37 (a) Top view showing tuning sequence and string sizes; (b) securing lower ends of strings.

be equalized approximately all round when the instrument is tuned.

The bridges

These are formed by resting the strings in the slots in the heads of the wood screws. It will be seen from Fig. 37(b) that the bridge screws are inclined at an angle of approximately 15° from the perpendicular, towards their respective ends of the strut. The holes for these screws should be drilled to a depth of 15 mm, using an $\frac{1}{8}$ in. drill.

Tighten the screws until their heads are at the correct heights of 10 mm and 15 mm from the strut, with their slots parallel to the direction of the strings.

The hitch-pins

Drive 1 in. nails into the places marked, inclining them the same way as the bridge screws, but this time about 30° from the perpendicular. Leave half of each nail protruding, and cut off the head 10 mm from the wood, using a miniature hack-saw. The burr should be filed off, to enable the 'barrels' on the ends of the strings to fit easily over the nails.

The wrest-pins

The holes for these are drilled at right angles to the strut, 15 mm deep, using a $\frac{5}{32}$ in. drill, which is just large enough to enable the bolts to form threads in the wood as they are screwed in.

The bolts have $\frac{1}{16}$ in. holes drilled through their shanks just below the heads, to take the strings (Fig. 39). The drilling of these small holes is not difficult if tackled systematically, as follows:— The first thing is to make sure you are not confusing the 2 BA bolts with the $\frac{3}{16}$ in. Whitworth ones, which look rather similar (unless you are using brass bolts for the wrest-pins).

Drill a $\frac{5}{32}$ in. hole in a spare piece of wood, and screw in a bolt until about 15 mm still shows. Clamp it in a vice, with the head of the bolt resting against one of the jaws for support (see Fig. 39). File a small 'flat' where the hole is to be, and punch the exact place sharply, once, with a centre punch and a light hammer. This forms a small depression, which should be enough to prevent the drill from wandering when you begin to drill the hole.

Use a sharp, preferably new, $\frac{1}{16}$ in. high-speed twist drill. Angle the drill carefully so that the hole

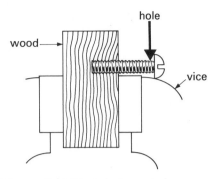

Fig. 39 Support for drilling holes in wrest-pins.

is central in the shank of the bolt, which will otherwise be weakened. It is essential to drill in a steady, relaxed and unhurried manner. Just a little too much pressure or wobble will result in an expensive crop of broken drills and a great deal of frustration. An effective way to keep a hand-drill steady is to rest your chin on the hand which is holding the top of the handle. With practice, these holes can be drilled at the rate of about one a minute, but it is wise to go very slowly at first.

Steel bolts will eventually rust in the wood, especially if the instrument is out of use for any length of time. Rusting can be delayed considerably by the application of a little grease to the threads before they are screwed in. With the very fine threads of conventional zither pins, this might well cause slipping, but with the relatively coarse thread we are using, it will not. Furthermore, any tendency to unwind when the string is tensioned can be counteracted by tightening the nut down on to the wood. For this reason, and to give added lateral support against the pull of the strings, the nuts should be put on to the bolts before they are screwed into place. When the bolts have been tightened to their working position, with their heads about 15 mm above the wood of the strut, the nuts can be screwed down finger-tight against the wood, as shown in the diagram on p. 48 (Fig. 42).

Fine-tuners

These will amply repay the time and trouble spent in making them. They work as shown in Fig. 41

Fig. 38 Coke-hod dulcimer showing the wrest-pins, wing-nut tuners and bridge screws.

Fig. 40 Drilling a $\frac{1}{16}$ in. hole in a bolt for use as a wrest-pin.

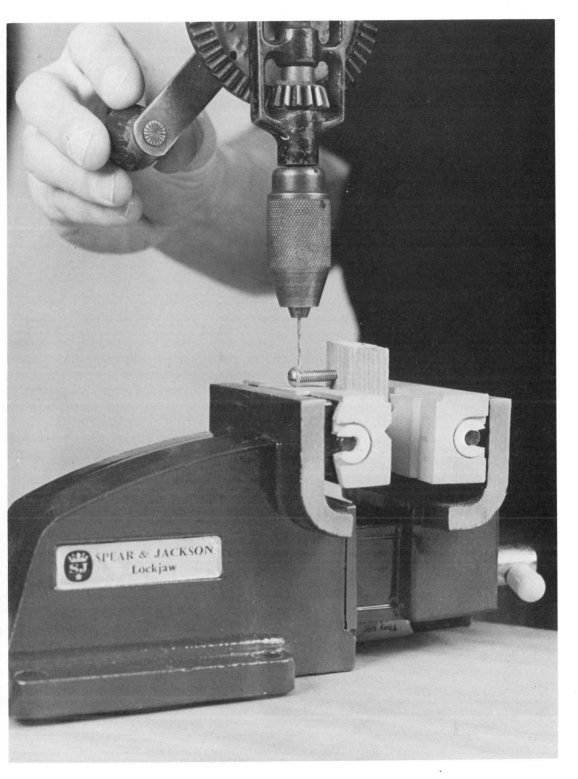

and make precise tuning a very simple matter.

To make a tuner, screw a $\frac{3}{16}$ in. Whitworth threaded bolt into a $\frac{5}{32}$ in. hole in a spare piece of wood, as for the wrest pins, but leaving 12 mm of the thread projecting, and this time placing it upright in the vice. Saw the head off as near as possible to the top of the shank, and then cut a slot lengthwise, down to within 1 mm of the wood. Some care is needed to keep the slot straight and central. If it wanders, a piece of the bolt may break off. The sawing is best done with a miniature hacksaw, except for the tuners which are to take the No. 4 sized guitar strings. These are thicker, and they will be too tight a fit in their slots unless a full sized hack-saw blade is used. Even more care will then be needed to keep the slots straight and central. If the task seems too difficult, a simple solution is to use $\frac{1}{4}$ in. bolts and wing nuts for the larger strings, but it is possible with the $\frac{3}{16}$ in. bolts (for $\frac{1}{4}$ in. bolts drill $\frac{7}{32}$ in. diameter holes).

When the slot has been cut, any burr at the top of the thread should be very gently removed with a small file, and a wing nut screwed down on to the slotted bolt. A small screwdriver is used to remove the tuner from its temporary piece of wood, *supporting the slotted part at the top by leaving the wing nut there during the process.* (Otherwise the slot will be opened out and the tuner broken.) If the wing nut has closed the slot, the screwdriver may have to be slightly sharpened, so as to open it up again.

The holes for the tuners are drilled exactly as for the wrest-pins; that is to say, perpendicular to the strings, 15 mm deep, and $\frac{5}{32}$ in. in diameter.

When screwing in a tuner, leave the wing nut in place, and continue gently until the bottom of the slot is almost level with the surface of the wood,

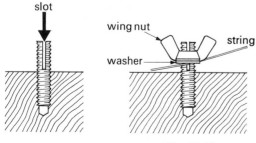

Fig. 41 Fine tuners.

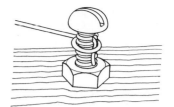

Fig. 42 String anchorage in wrest-pin bolt.

and parallel to the strings. Remember to grease the thread slightly first. The wing nut can then be removed and put aside until the strings are fitted.

Stringing

To fit a string, proceed as follows:

(a) Slide the 'barrel' at the lower end of the string over the hitch-pin, pressing it down as far as it will go.

(b) Pass the other end through its hole in the wrest-pin.

(c) Place the string in its slot in the fine-tuner.

(d) Pull up almost all the slack (the correct amount can only be learned by experience) and bend the end of the string down hard at the point where it emerges from the wrest-pin.

(e) Tighten with a large screwdriver (clockwise), pressing the string downwards into the screw threads of the wrest-pin bolt, and allowing it to pass round its own end where it was bent down, as shown in Fig 42.

(f) Cut off the spare end of the string with wire cutters or metal shears.

(g) Lift the string into the slots of the bridge screws, and take up any remaining slackness by tightening further, still pressing the string downwards.

(h) Place a flat washer and a wing nut on top of the string where it passes through the slot in the fine-tuner, and screw it down just far enough to stop the washer rattling.

Precautions

Fit and tighten the strings on *alternate* sides of the strut.

BEWARE OF PAINFUL PUNCTURES IN THE FINGERS WHICH CAN BE INFLICTED BY THE VERY SHARP ENDS OF STEEL GUITAR STRINGS.

Preliminary tuning

In case of mishaps, the initial tuning should be done before the coke-hod, or other resonating box, is attached. The strings are tuned to the notes specified in the stringing plan (Fig. 36). A piano, chime bars, or a glockenspiel would be a useful guide. Use a large screwdriver to turn the wrest-pin bolts, and pull the strings up slowly to somewhere near their eventual pitch, beginning with the lowest note (C), and working up the scale. Do not use the fine tuners at this stage.

One or two things may now go wrong. If the barrels at the lower ends of the strings have not been pushed right down on the hitch pins, the nails will bend, and the strings will fly off. If a string has not been pulled far enough through the hole in its wrest-pin bolt before wrapping it round, the bolt may jam in its hole while the string is still below pitch. If the bridge screws slope back too far, the sharp edges of their slots may eventually cut through the strings. Two or three strokes with a small mousetail file will cure this tendency. The solutions to the other problems are fairly simple. It may be necessary to replace a hitch-pin, or to shorten the end of a string.

The resonating box

As soon as all is reasonably secure, and no strings appear to be flying about, attention can be turned to the resonating box. You may not be able to buy a new coke-hod, but an old one, scrubbed out and painted, will do just as well. It need not be plastic. A laminated wooden one is even better. A galvanized metal one will also work, but is rather harsh and cumbersome. If you decide to make or adapt any other sort of box, it should be not much more than half the height of the strut, and have ample resonating surfaces. The effect of first plucking the strings without a resonator, and again with the strut held against various surfaces and containers, is quite surprising, and is a useful guide when selecting a container. If you can find nothing suitable, why not make your own?

Plywood resonating box

This can be made quite simply from gaboon plywood. The base is a 20 cm (8 in.) square, cut from a piece 12 mm ($\frac{1}{2}$ in.) thick. The sides, shaped as shown, are 6 mm ($\frac{1}{4}$ in.) thick, and the back and front, 4 mm ($\frac{3}{16}$ in.).

The two side pieces are planed together, to ensure that they are equal and have straight edges. They are then panel-pinned and glued to the base. The back and front edges of the base are planed to the slope of the back and front of the box. The other two pieces are then pinned and glued to the base, and to the edges of the side pieces. Care is needed to tap the panel pins in straight and centrally, so that they do not split the edges out. One method is to drill $\frac{1}{16}$ in. holes a little of the way first, remembering that such small drills are easily broken.

The box should be rubbed down, and painted or varnished. For painting, a sealing coat of emulsion paint or other primer will be necessary. The strut is secured inside this box with two screws, as shown in the drawing. A carrying handle can be fitted to the back of the box.

If all else fails, at least you will now have a coke-hod!

If you are using a plastic coke-hod, a $\frac{3}{16}$ in. hole should now be drilled in it just below the centre of the highest part of the rim, to take a screw. Stand the strut of the instrument inside the hod, with its unstrung narrow edge against the hole, and mark the place on it for the screw. Drill a smaller hole in the centre of the thickness of the strut, at exactly that height.

To ensure a close fit inside the bottom of the hod, it may be necessary to cut a small piece off the lower end of the strut. When this is done, screw it in place, at the top, using a round-headed screw, and making sure that the strut is as far forward as it will go at the bottom, and vertical from the front view. Drill a $\frac{3}{16}$ in. hole through the base of the hod where the centre of the end of the strut rests, and a smaller hole in the strut at that point. Recess the hole in the hod with a handled countersink or a countersink bit, and use a countersunk screw, to avoid scratching the floor. Tighten both screws, and the dulcimer is complete, and ready to be carefully tuned.

If you are using any other sort of resonating box, the best method of securing the strut inside it will become evident when it is held in place.

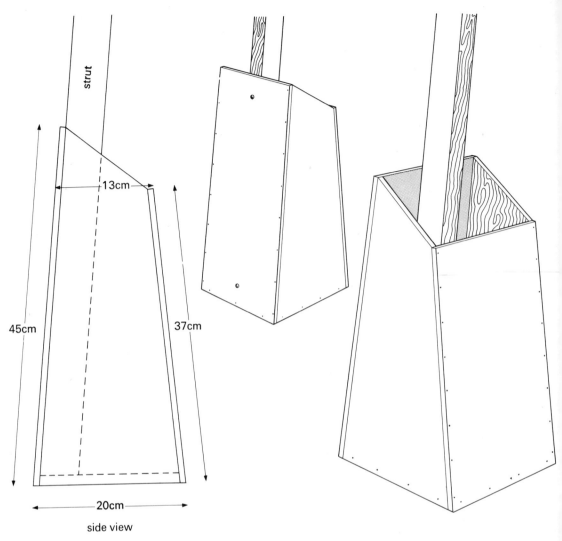

Fig. 43 Plywood resonating box for dulcimer.

Accurate tuning

Set the fine-tuners so that their washers are beginning to tighten the strings. Tune all the strings as carefully as possible by means of the wrest-pin bolts. Check that all their nuts are finger-tight against the wood. If any of the wrest-pins show signs of slipping, tighten the nuts with pliers or a spanner, just enough to secure them. Never try to force a wrest-pin round. If one begins to jam, it will have to be unscrewed far enough for some more of the string to be pulled through and bent down.

New strings, and a new instrument, will not stay in tune for long. The fine-tuners will make as much as a semitone difference, but their use should be kept to a minimum, and any sizeable adjustments made with a screwdriver. Everything will have settled down in a day or two, and the screwdriver should seldom be needed after that.

When slackening a fine-tuner to flatten a note, it is advisable to press down the sounding part of the string lightly with the finger, in case it is sticking on the bridge screws or in the slot of the tuner.

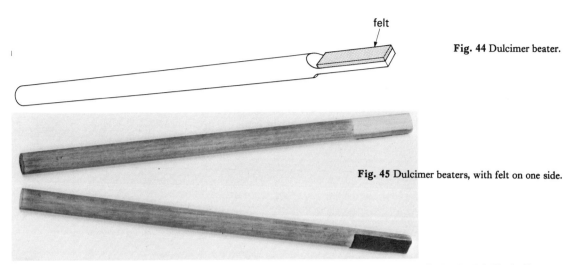

felt

Fig. 44 Dulcimer beater.

Fig. 45 Dulcimer beaters, with felt on one side.

Beaters

Dulcimer beaters are normally spade-shaped, with felt on one side. For the coke-hod dulcimer, it is very simple to make a pair of beaters from a piece of $\frac{1}{2}$ in. dowelling.

Cut two 10 in. lengths of dowel, and flatten the opposite sides of one end of each stick for about 2 in., with a file. Glue a strip of thin felt on to one of the flat sides of each stick (see Fig. 44).

Playing

The instrument can be held between the knees, with the bass (C) string either towards or away from the player. In the former position it will be found that the doh and soh chords are on the player's right hand side, and the fah chord is on the left. Other chords are also possible, but these three are the so-called 'primary triads', which form the basis of a great many traditional song accompaniments.

With a beater held lightly in each hand, it is possible to produce varied and interesting effects by tapping the strings singly or in pairs, sometimes with the felt side and sometimes with the wooden side.

A useful device for song accompaniments is the 'oom cha' or 'oom cha cha' figure, in which 'oom' represents the bass of the chord, and 'cha' the other notes above, sounded together.

In the key of C major, to which the dulcimer has so far been tuned, the notes of the primary chords are as follows:

doh C, E, G; soh G, B, D; fah F, A, C.

These chords are often referred to by the position in the scale of their principal note, or root. Thus, the doh chord is I, the fah chord is IV, and the soh chord is V. The seventh note above the root can be added to the V chord to give it some extra colour. In the key of C, this would be the note F.

Plucking

Further effects can be obtained by plucking the strings, either with the fingers alone, with or without the nails, or with a guitar plectrum in each hand, or with finger plectra. A plectrum which will last for a reasonable time can be made from a piece of rubber, leather, or even stiff card.

You will notice that the tone varies according to the part of the string which is plucked or struck, being more sonorous near the centre, and more strident near the bridge.

Bowing

This is normally easier when the bass string is on the side away from the player, although some may prefer it the other way round. Violin or cello bows, one held in each hand, enable melodies to be played, as well as sonorous three-part chords, sounding not unlike a mediaeval 'chest of viols'.

If the bows do not seem to grip the strings, some violin resin should help. In drawing out the tone with a bow, there is a knack which is acquired through practice.

Alternative tunings

Musicians will realize that appropriate notes can be sharpened or flattened, allowing the instrument to be played in various keys.

Here are some examples of alternative tunings:

(a) Change B to B flat (key of F major). The chords are now:

```
doh  F   A   C
soh  C   E   G    (B♭ optional)
fah  B♭  D   F
```

(b) Change B to B flat and E to E flat (key of B flat major). The chords are now:

```
doh  B♭  D   F
soh  F   A   C    (E♭ optional)
fah  E♭  G   B♭
```

(c) Change F to F sharp (key of G major). The chords are now:

```
doh  G   B   D
soh  D   F♯  A    (C optional)
fah  C   E   G
```

(d) Change F to F sharp, and C to C sharp (key of D major). The chords are now:

```
doh  D   F♯  A
soh  A   C♯  E    (G optional)
fah  G   B   D
```

In these examples, the soh chord precedes the fah chord, as it is generally more prominent and frequent in occurrence.

N.B. If the instrument is to sound as it should, and these chords are to be effective, the importance of good tuning cannot be over-stressed. This is where the advantage of the fine-tuners becomes very obvious.

Now, if you have been successful with the coke-hod dulcimer, you may feel ready to try making a keyboard instrument. The simple keyed psalteries described in the next chapter use wrest-pins and fine-tuners identical to those in the dulcimer. They have chromatic keyboards, and a simplified version of the action of a traditional spinet or harpsichord. They can be made entirely from materials which are either reclaimed or bought locally, and they cost only a fraction of what would normally be expected for instruments of this type. Their construction calls for some patience and perseverance, but it is not really difficult. To play on a keyboard instrument of authentic sound quality—one which you have made yourself—is a uniquely rewarding experience.

Fig. 46 Playing the coke-hod dulcimer with beaters.

Fig. 47 (*overleaf*) Harmony with two bows.

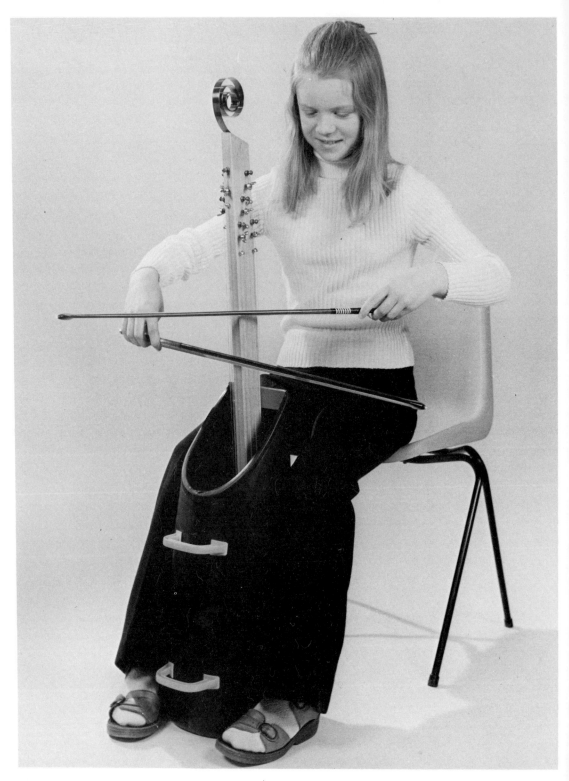

6 Keyed pralteries

The black and white pattern of the piano keys is so familiar to us, that we seldom stop to think about its origins, or how intriguing the notion of making a stringed instrument operated by finger levers must once have been. It seems to have been applied first to a monochord, probably in the eleventh or twelfth century A.D., incorporating an idea already used in the hurdy-gurdy. During the following three centuries it grew to resemble a kind of psaltery, with a keyboard similar to that of an organ.

The monochord, first used by the ancient Greeks for the scientific exploration of musical sounds, consisted of a single string stretched between two bridges on a long resonating box, with a third, movable bridge between the other two. The hurdy-gurdy was a relative of the vielles, or fiedels, which came to Europe from the near east in about the ninth century A.D., and which were early ancestors of the violin or fiddle family. The player of the hurdy-gurdy turns with his right hand the crank of a resined wheel which vibrates the strings, while his left hand operates finger keys which press wooden strips, or tangents, against the strings to sound different notes. The psaltery is a simple harp-like instrument in which the strings are stretched over a triangular or trapezoidal-shaped sounding box, and plucked with a plectrum, or with the fingers.

The organ is thought to have been invented in about 300 B.C., by an Egyptian physicist named Ctesibius. He used an ingenious system of water-powered air compression, which was why the Romans called the instrument a 'hydraulus'. Some examples had as many as twenty finger keys, each about two inches wide. Apart from its use of water, the hydraulus was remarkably like a small pipe organ of later times, although by some accounts it was considerably louder. The Emperor Nero is said to have been an expert performer on this instrument.

Probably because of the way the Romans treated them, the early Christians were slow to introduce the organ into their religious services. When they eventually did so, it was very similar to the Roman instrument, except that it used foot-operated bellows instead of water to provide the wind pressure. By the tenth century A.D. the largest instruments, like the famous one at Winchester, had reached monumental size, with as many as four hundred pipes, needing seventy men to operate the bellows, and the whole of the player's fist to depress the keys.

At the other extreme were the small 'portative' organs, sometimes slung round the neck of the player, who would work the bellows with one hand and the keys with the other. It was from these smaller instruments that the size of the keys became more or less standardized, by about the end of the fourteenth century. At first there were only what we should call the 'white' notes. With the development of musical composition came the need for semitones, and so pieces were cut out between the keys in the appropriate places, and shorter lengths inserted. The first to be used was B flat, enabling the player to avoid the 'augmented fourth' from F to B natural, which was regarded as ugly. Next came F sharp, probably followed by E flat, then C sharp, and finally G sharp. This was no easy or obvious development, because it posed serious problems of tuning. For example, D sharp and E flat are not really quite the same note, and to the sensitive ear the idea of forcing one semitone key to split the difference and serve both purposes was obnoxious. The problem was eventually resolved in the seventeenth century, by the division of the octave into twelve equal semitones, a solution which still offends the ears of some purists, but was happily accepted by no less a musician that Johann Sebastian Bach. He composed his 'Well-tempered Clavier', the famous set of forty-eight preludes and fugues, one in every key, to show how well this system of 'equal temperament' could work.

So, four hundred years before the pianoforte began to establish itself, the familiar pattern of twos and threes, which most of us automatically associate with that instrument, was evolved. The really astonishing thing is that the keyboard has remained totally unchanged, apart from small variations in size, and the swopping of colours between naturals and sharps, since 1450, and this despite enormous developments in the demands made upon it. One reason is that it is a highly effective tool, which influenced the subsequent course of musical composition. Another is that its mastery demands so many hours of dedicated practice, that performers have always become highly resistant to any suggested improvements, however logical these might be. Imagine the outcry from typists if all their keyboards were to be rearranged!

The mechanism mentioned above, which was adapted from the hurdy-gurdy and applied to the monochord, was a very simple one, but so effective that it remained in constant use for over four hundred years, and has been revived in the present century. The instrument came to be called a 'clavichord', from the Latin *clavis*—a key. On one end of a pivoted lever is a brass blade, or tangent. When the other end is pressed down, the tangent touches the string, sounding a gentle note whose pitch depends mainly on the position of the point of contact along the string, but also to a certain extent on the amount of pressure applied to the lever. Thus a slight vibrato is possible, as well as some variation in volume. If one end of the string is permanently 'damped' with cloth or felt, only a single note will sound, and all will be silent again as soon as the key is released. This was the basis for a very soft-toned, intimate and expressive instrument.

Eventually, extra strings were added, enabling more than one note to be sounded at a time. By the early fifteenth century there were clavichords with chromatic keyboards of three octaves, and as many as ten strings. Groups of adjacent semitones would normally share a string, being seldom required to sound together in the music of that period. The next development was to double each string, for extra sonority, and to extend the compass to four octaves. In this form the instrument achieved very wide popularity, being compact, quickly tuned, and cheap to make. By the eighteenth century, still larger clavichords were being made, with a pair of strings for every note. Some were even made with pedal keyboards like an organ.

The style of composition which developed from such an expressive instrument prepared the way for the introduction of the new 'fortepiano'. By the end of the eighteenth century this had become recognized as being far more suitable for ensemble use, having a much greater dynamic range. Within a very short time the charming little clavichord was almost completely forgotten, and its re-emergence had to wait for another century.

The other ancestors of the pianoforte, the harpsichords, spinets and virginals, were grander and more powerful in tone than the clavichord, but less able to respond to the player's touch. These instruments really came into their own during the sixteenth century, although examples are known to have existed earlier. The names of the various members of the family have been somewhat loosely applied. Generally, the instrument whose strings are parallel to the keys is called a harpsichord, the oblong one a virginal, and the harp-shaped or polygonal one a spinet. Harpsichords often have more than one set of strings, with mechanisms for varying their tone colours and registration. However, all the members of this group employ the same kind of plucking device.

Resting on the further end of each key is a rod, or jack, which is able to slide up and down in slotted guides. Near the top of the jack is a small pivoted tongue, held in line with the jack against a stop, by a hair spring. Hog bristle was traditionally used for this. A piece of hard leather, or else crow quill, nowadays replaced by Delrin plastic, projects from the tongue, and plucks the string as soon as the key is pressed down. On release, it falls back past the string again, with a small but characteristic sound. A felt damper, slotted into the top of the jack, touches the string while the key is at rest.

Very few of the books which describe this action explain how it is that the plectrum is able to pluck the string in one direction, and to slide past it in the other. In fact it is a simple and ingenious form of escapement, operating by leverage around a fulcrum. The relative positions of the plucking point and the pivot, together with the scope of the movement of the tongue, cause the return of the plectrum to tilt the tongue back against its spring, whereas the plucking movement holds it in its original position.

Making keyboard instruments

At first, the idea of making a keyboard instrument may seem daunting, in view of the sheer number of parts, and their apparent complexity. There certainly is a fair amount of repetitive work involved, needing time and patience, but there is really nothing very difficult about it. Simple homemade jigs will speed up the work and ensure accuracy. It is possible to make quite a handsome instrument without anything as complicated as a dovetail or even a mortice joint. Beginners can go ahead with some confidence after a little instruction in the basic uses of tools. All the necessary techniques are described in books on elementary woodworking, or else may be learned at evening classes. They will obviously have many useful applications besides the making of instruments.

The following are the main requirements: you should be able to measure and mark out accurately; to plane a piece of wood straight and flat with any two adjacent surfaces at right-angles; to plane end-grain squarely without chipping off the edges; to use a hand drill steadily, holding it perpendicular to the work, and to make the right sized holes for screws so that they will tighten without splitting the wood; to saw close to a line; to clean out corners with a chisel; and lastly, but by no means least, to sharpen tools on an oilstone.

Shooting board

This is an almost indispensable item for the accurate planning of small parts. Assuming that you already have the use of a bench with a planing stop, a vice and a bench hook, its making will provide some useful practice in planing and squaring some boards. A convenient size for the base of the shooting-board would be about 20 in. by 8 in. (50 cm by 20 cm). If a wide enough board of good quality is not available, a piece of thick plywood, not less than 9 mm, will do. The top board should be about 5 in. (13 cm) wide, and 2 cm in thickness. The two boards may be screwed and glued together, with the heads of the screws countersunk well below the surface of the wood. The planing stop is made from an accurately squared piece of hardwood, 10 mm to 15 mm thick and about 4 cm wide. This is screwed and glued near the end of the top board, as illustrated in Fig. 48, using a set-square or a joiner's square to set it exactly at right-angles to the inner edge of the top board.

The shooting-board illustrated is made the normal way round for a right-handed user, but those who are left-handed will find it easier to use if the stop is at the other end.

To use the shooting-board, place the work against the stop, with the surface to be planed projecting very slightly over the edge of the top board. A smoothing plane, or a jack plane, well sharpened and finely set, is run on its side along the lower board, with its sole resting against the edge of the upper one. The work is held firmly against the stop, and moved fractionally towards the plane as each shaving comes off. A little linseed oil will protect the board from wear, and help the plane to run smoothly.

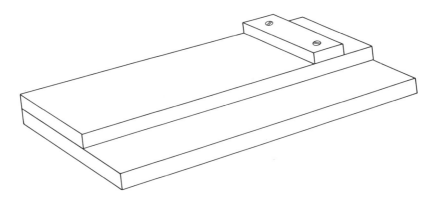

Fig. 48 Shooting-board.

As its name implies, the shooting board is mainly intended for accurately 'shooting', or squaring, the ends of pieces across the grain. When doing this, the further corner of the wood to be planed should be slightly bevelled with a chisel, to prevent the last piece of the grain from splitting out. The shooting board will also be found invaluable, however, for planing and squaring small pieces of wood with the grain, and particularly for making straight edges and right-angled corners in plywood, which should always be sawn on the large side, as it is liable to crumble even with a fine saw.

Simplified keyboard and harpsichord action

The method of making a keyboard described below is very simple and unorthodox, and would probably shock a maker of traditional instruments. It can be used for a simplified form of harpsichord action, combining the jack, tongue and spring in one piece, screwed to the underside of the key. It is suitable for fitting to the top of a psaltery, since the plucking movement is downwards, unlike that of the traditional instrument. It can also be used for a version of the clavichord action.

During the process of making this system work satisfactorily, I encountered a great many unforeseen snags and difficulties. Solutions eventually appeared, and the result was surprising and delightful. As remarked earlier, it is just this sort of experimenting, more than anything else, which can give some idea of the sense of excitement, discovery, frustration and eventually success, which our predecessors must have felt when these instruments were first being invented.

No particular advantage is claimed for this action, apart from its simplicity of construction, and the fact that there are fewer parts to wear out. Its main justifications are that it can be made from odd scraps of whatever is lying about or may be bought from the local shops, and that it really does work.

The simplified keyboard is made from a single piece of 4 mm gaboon plywood, selected carefully to avoid uneven or broken grain. It is cut like a large comb, with the surface grain at right-angles to the keys, which allows more vertical and less lateral movement. The key fronts, naturals and sharps, are glued in place on the ends of the 'teeth' of the comb. The key movement is provided by the springiness of the plywood, which hardly has to bend at all to allow a touch depth of about 8 mm. After each key has been secured with two screws at its far end to a transverse rail, the whole board is cut into separate pieces, so that individual keys can be removed for adjustments to the action, or the

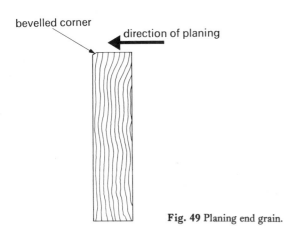

bevelled corner

direction of planing

Fig. 49 Planing end grain.

Fig. 50 A model of the action of the keyed psaltery.

replacement of parts. The plywood is treated with linseed oil, which makes it more supple and durable, as well as enhancing its appearance. The touch weight can be adjusted by placing small packing pieces between the keys and the rail.

The jack is made from a piece of Atomic copper weather strip, which is stocked by most hardware shops, and has just the right degree of springiness. A plectrum cut from shoe leather is glued into a hole in the jack. The mechanism is sprung gently against an adjustable cam, screwed into a strip of wood above the soundboard of the instrument.

The damper is separate from the jack, and consists of a 6BA bolt, carrying a small felted plastic strip, screwed into a block under the key. This enables the keyboard to be levelled, by screwing the damper in or out.

A model of the action

Before attempting to build a keyboard instrument of any kind, the beginner is strongly advised to make a model of the action, either based on a monochord with a single key, or with a pair of strings and keys.

To make a monochord with this action, the following materials are needed:

A piece of wooden batten, approximately 5 cm by 2 cm, and at least 30 cm long.

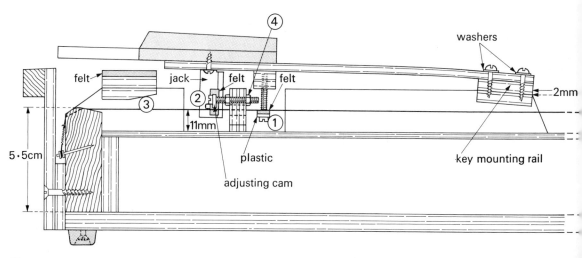

A piece of 6 mm plywood, 30 cm by 10 cm.

A piece of 4 mm gaboon plywood, 20 cm by 1·4 cm, with the surface grain across the length.

A few small pieces of wood for key rails, covering, etc.

A hitch-pin and a wrest-pin (*see* Chapter 5).

A steel guitar string; 1st, 2nd or 3rd.

Two 6BA bolts; one inch long, with nuts.

Round-headed wood screws; two of each, half-inch No. 4, and three-eighths inch No. 2.

Atomic weather strip (draught excluder for door frames etc.).

A small quantity of tough leather, such as shoe leather, about $\frac{1}{4}$ in. thick (an old, hard leather belt could be used).

Some thin felt.

A short piece of the plastic water piping as used for the treble flute (*see* Chapter 4), or any tough, resilient plastic about 2 mm thick.

Fast-setting epoxy adhesive.

This may appear to be a rather formidable list, but it contains a little of almost everything needed to make a complete keyboard instrument.

The first thing is to make an accurate full-sized drawing of the action, as seen from one side, on the piece of 6 mm plywood, which is then cut to shape. The batten can be nailed and glued in position on the plywood, and the bridges glued in place. Holes are drilled for the wrest-pin and the hitch-pin, and these are fitted as shown. Short sections of the key rails and the jack rail can also be pinned and glued in position on the plywood. Notice that the jack rail

has two holes drilled through it; one $\frac{1}{4}$ in. in diameter for the string to pass through, and the other $\frac{3}{32}$ in., to take the screw of the adjusting cam. The steel guitar string can now be fitted, and tightened until it sounds a clear note when plucked.

Before going any further, it is worthwhile checking all the measurements again carefully. These have been arrived at after a considerable amount of experiment, and should result in an action which sounds and feels very similar to that of a normal harpsichord. The height of the bridge and the nut are important in relation to the height of the key rails and the length of the jack. The exact position of the plectrum on the jack has a marked effect on the touch. The length and thickness of the key affect its lateral stability and the touch weight. A longer key would tend to twist in its length and wobble sideways, while a shorter one would feel unpleasantly springy, and might eventually break off in use. Notice that the rail to which the key is screwed slopes down by 2 mm towards the wrest-pin, to provide enough spring for the return of the key.

The key

This can be either a sharp or a natural. The measurements are shown in the keyboard plan (Fig. 58). The back end, made from the narrow strip of 4 mm plywood, is identical in either case. A cover for the natural key, adequate for this model of the action, can be cut from a piece of 4 mm or

Fig. 51 Keyed psaltery, sectional view from side showing assembly of parts. The damper screw (1) is adjusted so that the plectrum (2) rests just above its strings before the keys are pressed, and so that the keyboard is level; (3) chamfer to allow for cam adjustment from front; (4) tightening nut for adjusting cam screw. Height of bridge 1·2 cm, string height 1·1 cm.

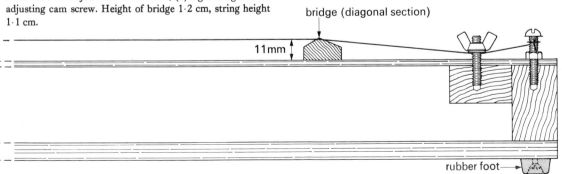

bridge (diagonal section)

11mm

rubber foot

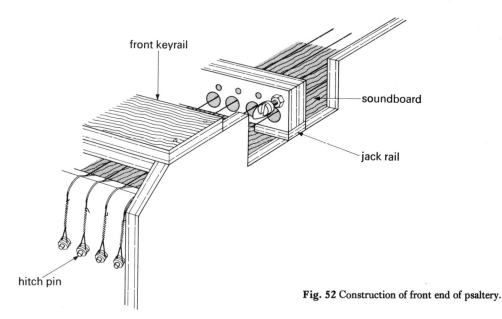

front keyrail

soundboard

jack rail

hitch pin

Fig. 52 Construction of front end of psaltery.

6 mm plywood, with the grain longways. A sharp key can be sawn, planed and sanded from any suitable slip of wood, or made simply from a piece of thick plywood on its edge. Two pieces of 6 mm plywood glued together will do quite well.

To glue the cover on to the key, first scrape a few shallow grooves under it with a sharp knife or a chisel. Mark its position on the back end of the key, and press it firmly in place, using fast-setting epoxy adhesive. Stand a weight on it for about ten minutes, checking that it is still in position. Meanwhile, two thin layers of felt should be glued on the top of the front key rail, to absorb the thump of the key.

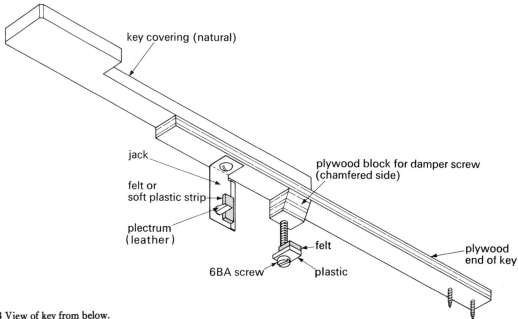

key covering (natural)

jack

felt or soft plastic strip

plectrum (leather)

plywood block for damper screw (chamfered side)

6BA screw

felt

plastic

plywood end of key

Fig. 53 View of key from below.

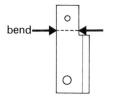

Fig. 54 The jack before bending.

The jack

Cut off 3·5 cm of the Atomic weather strip, and divide it in half lengthways. Use the half which does not have the pin holes marked on it. It can be cut easily with metal shears or tough scissors. Lay the piece down with its wrapped over edge on the right-hand side, facing towards you. Mark a small rectangle in the top right hand corner, 12 mm from the top and 4 mm wide, as shown, and snip this piece out, being careful not to cut too far. If this corner is left on, the jack will be too stiffly sprung, while if the whole of the wrapped over edge is cut off, it will be too flexible.

Next, punch the places for the two holes, which should be accurately marked. The one at the narrow end is drilled $\frac{3}{32}$ in., and the other one $\frac{1}{8}$ in. Use a sharp drill, with very little pressure and support the jack in the angle of a bench hook, otherwise the metal may suddenly twist itself around the drill. Push the end of the jack at right angles over the end of a piece of wood, in the direction shown, exactly 2 cm from the centre of the larger hole. It may need bending a little more with pliers afterwards.

The plectrum

The leather should be chopped on a piece of flat hardwood, using a very sharp knife. Cut a tapering wedge, 1 cm long, and 4 mm at its wider end. Push it through the $\frac{1}{8}$ in. hole in the jack, in the direction shown, and form a dome of quick-setting epoxy adhesive over its outer end. Make sure that the bottom edge of the plectrum is perpendicular to the

face of the jack. While the glue hardens, rest the jack over a strip of wood, with the glued side uppermost. The glue will then flow into the desired shape, and can later be chiselled away from the jack if the plectrum needs replacing.

Trim the point of the plectrum to the shape illustrated in Fig. 55, so that it projects no more than 5 mm from the jack. Harpsichord makers would regard this shape as rather thick and stumpy, needing very precise adjustment, and allowing for no free play in the parts. However, the sprung action described here permits such fine adjustment, and the thicker plectrum gives a slightly louder tone, compensating somewhat for the small soundboards of the psalteries.

The damper

This is screwed into a square of 9 mm plywood, glued to the underneath of the key in the position shown. Notice that one side of the plywood slopes, from the front view, to leave room for the adjacent key to be removed if necessary. A $\frac{3}{32}$ in. hole is drilled 3 mm from the other side, 1 cm deep, and perpendicular to the surface of the key, to take the one inch 6BA screw which carries the damper.

A piece is cut from the plastic piping, or similar material, 9 mm by 7 mm. A $\frac{3}{32}$ in. hole is drilled near one end of this, and the plastic is screwed all the way on to the 6BA screw, until it is tight against the head. Two small pieces of thin felt, or one piece of thicker felt, are then glued to the plastic where it will touch the string. Finally the damper is screwed into its block under the key until the head of the screw is 18 mm from the wood.

Fig. 55 Plectrum shape.

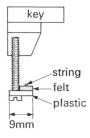

Fig. 56 Damper (front view).

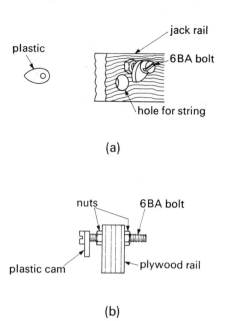

(a)

(b)

Fig. 57 Fitting of adjusting cams (before stringing).

The adjuster

The cam for this is made from a piece of the same plastic as the damper. Its initial size is 6 mm by 1 cm. It is screwed firmly against the head of a No. 6BA bolt, 1 in. long. The plastic is then cut and filed to the egg-shape shown in Fig. 57. The adjuster is screwed into its $\frac{3}{32}$ in. hole in the jack rail, with a nut on either side of the rail. These nuts are tightened towards each other until the adjuster will only turn fairly stiffly (see Fig. 57(b)).

Assembling the parts

The jack is screwed into the centre line of the underneath of the key, 1·5 cm from the front end of the plywood part, using a $\frac{3}{8}$ in. round-headed wood screw, size 2, for which a $\frac{1}{16}$ in. hole is drilled, 8 mm deep. The jack is tightened facing the same way round as the damper.

The key should now be screwed to its mounting rail, using two $\frac{1}{2}$ in. size 4 round-headed wood screws, preferably brass or chromium. Care is needed to ensure that the key is parallel to the string. If the holes are drilled $\frac{5}{32}$ in., a little scope for adjustment is provided. The damper should be under the string, and the adjusting cam turned to its least effective position.

It may now be necessary to remove the key

again, and screw the damper up or down, until it allows the point of the plectrum to stop on a level immediately above the top of the string, when viewed from the side. It may also be necessary to spring the jack across the line of the key, until the bottom of the plectrum rests on the top of the string, when the key is secured. The adjusting cam may now be turned clockwise, from the front view, while the key is pressed repeatedly, until a clear note sounds, with no more resistance than a slight 'ping' near the top of the key's descent.

If the plectrum fails to return to its starting position when the key is released, it may be because the damper is still slightly too close to the string, or there may be too little spring in the key itself. This can be cured by putting a small packing piece, such as a slip of the copper weather trip, under the key, by the front one of its two securing screws. When adjusted correctly, the touch should be light and pleasant, and the action should repeat at any speed without noticeable deterioration. If it feels too springy, a packing piece may be put by the back screw. The correct touch depth, that is, the distance moved by the front end of the key when pressed, is 7 to 8 mm. It will be obvious that this depends on the relative heights of the damper, the plectrum and the felt on the front rail.

A trio of keyed psalteries

Having made a successful working model of the action, it is time to consider possible layouts for a complete instrument. Many designs are feasible, but the one suggested here has several advantages. It consists of a simple chromatic psaltery with either seventeen or nineteen notes, and is made so that the keyboard comes right to its edges. This means that another similar instrument, continuous in pitch from the first one, can be placed alongside it to make a larger unit. In fact the total design includes three psalteries: a soprano, an alto and a bass. Placed together, these form a kind of simple harpsichord, with an inclusive compass of more than four octaves, from the C two octaves below middle C, to the E two octaves plus a major third above it. The bass and soprano instruments both have a seventeen note compass, from C to the E a tenth above, and the alto has nineteen notes, from the F below middle C to the B above it. This results

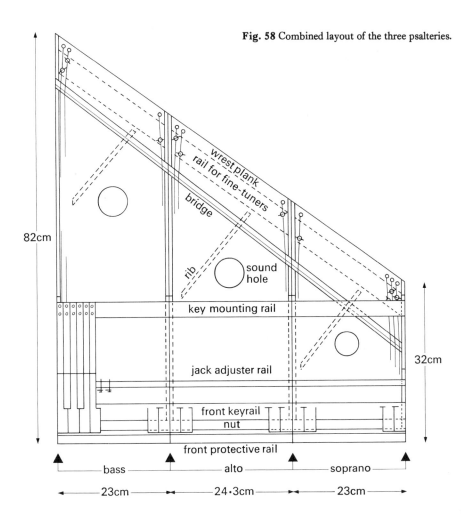

Fig. 58 Combined layout of the three psalteries.

82cm

wrest plank

rail for fine-tuners

bridge

rib

sound hole

key mounting rail

32cm

jack adjuster rail

front keyrail

nut

front protective rail

bass — alto — soprano

— 23cm — 24·3cm — 23cm —

in each section having a symmetrically patterned keyboard. The overall compass is sufficient for playing virtually all the music composed for keyboard instruments, other than the organ, up to the mid-eighteenth century, which includes among others everything of Scarlatti, Couperin, Handel and J.S. Bach.

From the beginner's point of view, there are several practical reasons for making an instrument in small sections. There is no need to embark on a seemingly endless task. No very large pieces of wood are needed, since there are three separate soundboards and frames. The resonating space under the soundboard of each section is reasonably appropriate to its own range of pitch. The instrument is easily portable in sections, and it can be

stowed compactly. The sections can be used separately by children, each playing a part of the same piece of music. If desired, it is not very difficult to make a case with a lid, a stand and a music desk, giving the combined instruments more than a passing resemblance to a small harpsichord.

All three sections are strung with steel guitar strings. These do not give such a good tone in the bass octave as would uncovered strings of much greater length, but they do provide a reasonable bass within a total length of less than three feet. Each string is fitted with a fine tuner, identical to the one described in Chapter 5 for the coke-hod dulcimer. This is a very great advantage with a chromatic instrument, since each note can be accurately tuned with little more than a flick of the

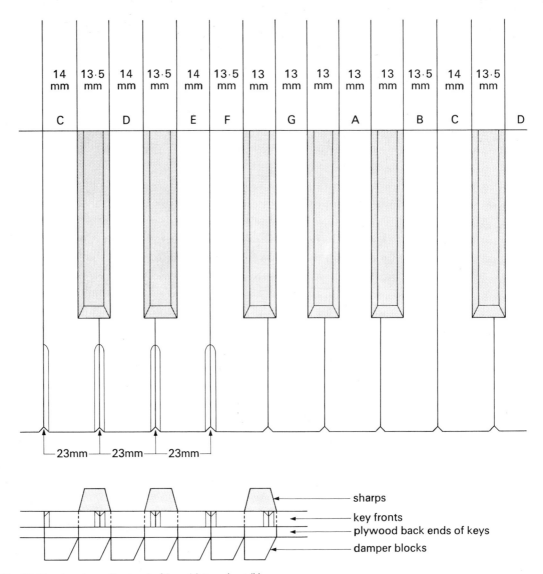

Fig. 59 Keyed psaltery; front end of keys (a) top view; (b) front view.

fingers. With these, and with the plectrum adjusters already described, two of the harpsichordist's recurring problems are considerably reduced.

Fig. 58 shows how the three instruments will combine to form a continuous unit. Notice that the wrest-pins and the bridge converge slightly towards the bass; that is, towards the player's left. This is so that the fine tuners can be fitted in behind the keyboard at the treble end, while saving

unnecessary length in the bass, and preserving a straight line along the back of the instrument for simplicity.

A keyboard plan

This is fascinating to draw, but not so straightforward as it may seem. As remarked earlier, the size of the keys has been more or less standardized for several centuries, but small variations are common.

The span per octave of twelve semitones, from C to B inclusive, is rarely less than 16 cm, or more than 16·5 cm. The hand readily adapts to this much variation. It is arithmetically impossible to divide the twelve semitones equally, and the seven naturals, and still preserve a straight division between E and F, since sevenths and twelfths of a unit do not coincide at any point. There are several ways out of this difficulty.

One way is to make all the naturals equal, and then to divide the span from C to E into five equal semitones, and that from F to B into seven. Another way is to make all the semitones equal, and to divide the two short spans so produced into three and four naturals, respectively. Various compromises are possible. It is interesting to measure the keys on a number of instruments, old and new. Irregularities will be found which are not at all obvious at first sight.

The layout suggested here adopts a span of 16·1 cm to the octave, which enables the front end of each natural to be 23 mm wide, before removing a wafer-thin shaving to allow free movement. The back ends of the keys are either 13 mm, 13·5 mm or 14 mm wide, before sawing. In no case is the back end of a sharp wider than that of an adjacent natural, since that would limit the space for large fingers between the sharps.

The measurements are set out in Fig. 59. A full-sized drawing is easily made using a drawing board, T-square, set-square and a metric ruler. It can be done on a table, using a set-square and a ruler, but inaccuracies are liable to creep in.

Working drawings

It is really essential to draw an accurate, full-sized plan, section and elevation of whichever one of the psalteries is being made. Otherwise time, wood and effort are very likely to be wasted, and enthusiasm blunted. Some may prefer to attempt the soprano member of the trio first, as it is the smallest. The other two are actually just as easy to make, but require more wood, including one extra piece of framing, to guard against any tendency to buckle under the tension of the strings. The most satisfying musically, on its own, is the alto, with nineteen semitones. Whichever one you decide upon, the drawing of the action should not present

any problem, if a successful working model has already been made.

In making the drawings, the following details should be noted carefully:

(a) The converging of the wrest-pins and bridge, already mentioned.
(b) The correct butting together of the framing pieces, for strength.
(c) The key rail mountings, enabling the keys to come right to the edges of the box, and the way this affects the positions of the two outer strings.
(d) The spacing of the wrest-pins and tuners, leaving room for the wing nuts to be turned.

A separate drawing should be made of the jack rail, to which the adjusting cams are screwed. The holes in this for the strings to pass through should be exactly in line with the centres of the keys, except for the two outer ones, which are drilled 2 mm further inwards. The strings are spaced in the same way.

Choice of wood

Reclaimed wood, from old furniture or an old piano, is always better than new wood, as long as it is free from woodworm or rot. If new wood has to be used, ramin, stocked by most timber yards, can be a useful substitute for some of the more expensive hardwoods. It varies in quality, and should feel fairly heavy, and have an even grain.

Framing pieces may be made from ramin, oak, beech, mahogany, spruce, or indeed almost any wood which is sound and well seasoned. The frames of the smaller instruments can be made entirely from thick plywood, or from thinner layers nailed and glued together.

Good quality soundboards are made of close-grained spruce. Many modern instruments, however, use thin plywood with a spruce veneer. For our purpose ordinary 3 mm gaboon ply is very satisfactory, being more resonant than birch ply, and having quite an attractive appearance. Marine quality plywood, used for boat building, is not usually resonant enough for a soundboard.

Oak should be avoided where steel nails or screws are to be used, as it contains a corrosive acid. Wrest planks (into which the wrest-pins are

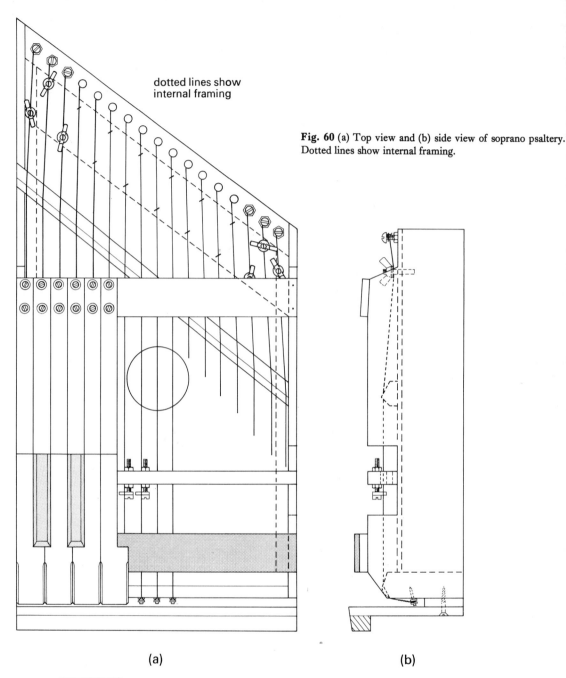

dotted lines show
internal framing

Fig. 60 (a) Top view and (b) side view of soprano psaltery. Dotted lines show internal framing.

(a)

(b)

screwed), bridges, and nuts are frequently made from beech, but any fairly hard and strong wood, including ramin, is suitable.

The keyboard, as already mentioned, is made of 4 mm gaboon ply, and the key coverings can be of any hardwood, with a contrasting colour for the

sharps. If you intend to make more than one of the psalteries, it is wise to ensure that enough of the same wood is available for all the key coverings. Many old instruments, as well as modern copies, have ebony naturals and lighter coloured sharps. Others again have boxwood or pearwood naturals and ebony sharps. Beechwood and mahogany make a very atttractive contrast either way round, especially if polished with a little linseed oil.

For those who may not care to saw and plane so many small slips of wood to size, there are some easy ways out. One is to cut the naturals from polished hardwood floor tiles, sold at DIY shops. Another is to buy some 1 in. by $\frac{1}{8}$ in. flat ramin strip, and reduce its width slightly to fit. This looks surprisingly good if carefully sanded, and oiled or varnished. The sharps can be of the same wood as the naturals, stained a different colour.

Adhesives

Hardware shops stock an ever-increasing range of adhesives, and it is quite interesting to test some of these by glueing scraps of wood, metal, plastics and fabric together with an assortment of brands, and finding out how easily they will come apart again. Some are definitely more versatile than others. For woodworking there is a wide choice. Evo-Stik Resin W is clean, easy to use and very strong. Cascamite is even stronger, but requires mixing. The new fast-setting epoxy adhesives will glue permanently almost anything, although they will sometimes break cleanly away from a smooth metallic surface. Some contact adhesives seem to stick more strongly to metal than others, if left long enough to set really hard.

Making the box

The woodwork is straightforward, and for that reason stands a better chance of being carried out accurately by a beginner than it would if it were more complicated. The close fitting of simple butted joints still adds considerably to their strength, even with modern space-filling glues.

All the joints should be panel-pinned and glued. Very few of the pin heads will show in the finished instrument, and those that do could be punched below the surface and covered with filler. The angled pieces for the sloping end need to be accurately marked with an adjustable bevel and a square, and sawn close to the lines.

The box is constructed on a floor of 9 mm plywood, extending its entire length, except for the front protective rail. The internal side frames, as well as the end pieces, are nailed and glued on top of the floor. Only the external side pieces, which support the key-rails, overlap the floor, and these should not be fitted until the soundboard has been glued in place.

It will be seen from the diagram that the end pieces (the wrest-plank and the hitch-pin rail) butt against the ends of the internal side frames. A further piece of wood, let into the tops of the side frames at the sloping end, is glued against the wrest-plank, immediately under the soundboard, to take the screws of the fine tuners. A piece of 9 mm plywood is fixed to the inner side of the hitch-pin rail, to support the front end of the sound-board, since the hitch-pin rail itself extends upwards to form the 'nut' over which the strings will pass.

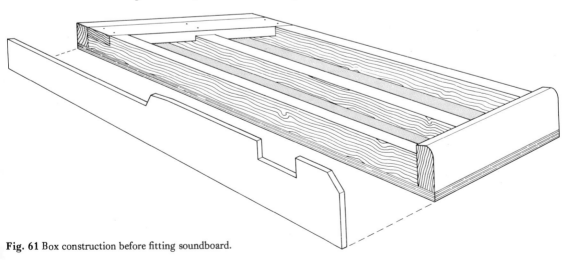

Fig. 61 Box construction before fitting soundboard.

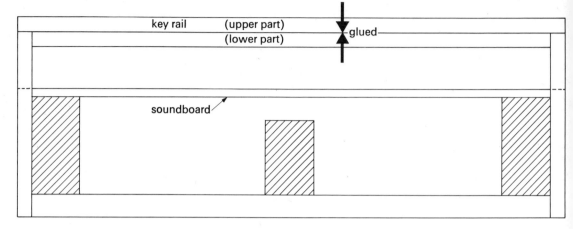

Fig. 62 Cross-section of soprano and bass psalteries; the internal frames shown are for the bass psaltery. (The alto psaltery is 23 mm wider.)

The boxes for the alto and bass sizes, being longer than the soprano, are therefore more liable to develop a slight upward curve towards their ends, under the tension of the strings. To counteract this, they have an additional central strut of spruce or hardwood, butted to the end pieces, and glued to the floor. It should be about 2 cm wide, and 3 cm in height, which leaves just sufficient clearance under the soundboard for a rib. For the same reason, the internal side frames of the alto psaltery should be one-and-a-half times as thick as those of the treble; and in the bass instrument, twice as thick. Suitable thicknesses would be 1 cm, $1\frac{1}{2}$ cm and 2 cm, respectively, bearing in mind that the outer side frames, glued on over their entire surface, also add strength.

Before any of the outermost pieces are fitted to the box, the surfaces to which they will be glued should be planed, if necessary, flat and true, inwards from the edges towards their centres.

The soundboard

This is made from a piece of 3 mm gaboon plywood (4 mm can be used), evenly grained, and free from blemishes or filler. As the edges are liable to crumble, even when cut with a fine saw held lightly and obliquely, it should be sawn 5 mm too large all round, and planed accurately to size. The surface grain should run parallel to the strings.

The sound hole, which is 5 cm in diameter in the treble psaltery and 6 cm in the others, can be cut very neatly with a partially home-made tool. The stock is removed from a cutting gauge, and a hole drilled through the shaft, 2·5 cm from the cutter for the treble size, and 3 cm for the others. The correct circle is drawn on the soundboard, and a thicker board, larger than the circle, is nailed to the underneath with four or five nails spaced inside the circle. A screw is passed through the hole in the shaft and into the centre of the circle. The cutter is then rotated clockwise, slowly and carefully, several times, until it has cut right through the plywood. The nailed on disc should then drop away with the board underneath it. It is a good idea to practise this on a spare piece of plywood first. The cutter needs to be well sharpened.

If you have no cutting gauge, a fret saw may be used, with the blade inserted through a small pilot hole.

The bridge, rib and nut

The bridge is made from close-grained hardwood, preferably beech, planed to the section shown. It should overlap the soundboard by fully 1 cm at each end, except on the short side of the soprano psaltery, since it has to come right to the edges of the external side frames. It can be planed down to its exact length after these have been fitted. A few shallow grooves should be scored on its underside before it is glued in place on the soundboard. It can

Fig. 63 Bridge cross-section.

1·2 cm

be clamped while the glue sets, by placing some strips of wood on top of it and standing weights on them.

The rib is glued to the underneath of the soundboard, crossing the line of the bridge, to help it to withstand the downward pressure of the strings. It stops just short of the frames of the box, so as not to restrict the freedom of vibration of the soundboard. Its position, from above, is shown in Fig. 58 by dotted lines. It can be made of close-grained spruce, or hardwood, about 1 cm square in section, but not so thick as to touch the central framing strut, in either of the two large instruments. It should taper somewhat from below towards its ends, giving it a fish-bellied shape (Fig. 64).

The nut is the rail over which the strings pass at their hitch-pin ends. In this design it is an upward extension of the hitch-pin rail, which forms the whole front of the box. The top is rounded, on the side away from the soundboard, as illustrated in Fig. 61, and the inner edge slopes downwards. The exact positions for the strings are marked on it, and each one is given a very fine and shallow groove, using a small triangular file on edge, or a miniature hack-saw. The grooves should be made entirely in the rounded section, finishing level with the top of the rail, so that a clean, sharp edge is presented to the strings, and so that they will all be on the same level.

The soundboard, with its bridge and rib, may now be glued in place on top of the side frames and the end piece, butting closely against the hitch-pin rail. If necessary it should be planed to a flush fit all along the other three sides. It can be clamped between strips of wood while glueing, or panel-pinned along its edges.

The external side frames

These are cut from 6 mm plywood, with the surface grain running lengthwise. They overlap the edges of the floor, and are level with the top of the soundboard from the key mounting rail to the wrest-plank. This means that they fit exactly under the ends of the bridge, except on the shorter side of the soprano psaltery, where the bridge is under the keyboard. The height of the key rail supports is important. So also is the slight backward slope of the mounting rail, which imparts just enough spring to the keys. Notice (Figs 51 and 61) the rectangular openings in the sides, which are cut as far down as the soundboard, to leave room for the action of the highest and lowest notes.

The side pieces should be glued over the whole of their area of contact with the box, and clamped or pinned in place.

The key rails

These are each made from two strips of 6 mm plywood, 3 cm wide, well glued together; the lower piece being 6 mm shorter at each end than the higher one. This produces the lapped joints, as shown in Fig. 65, to fit over the side pieces. The surface grain of each strip should go longways; that is, across the instrument. The rails are pinned and glued in place. A slight chamfer under the rear edge of the front rail (see Fig. 51) makes it easier to adjust the cams with a screwdriver.

The jack rail

Notice that this stands on a 'foot' at each end, made from a small piece of 4 mm plywood, to avoid contact with the soundboard except at the edges, so as to minimize the resonance of the noise of the action on the soundboard. The holes for the strings to pass through are drilled $\frac{1}{4}$ in. in diameter, and the ones to take the cam adjuster screws, $\frac{3}{32}$ in. The rail is made from a piece of 9 mm plywood, and is

soundboard

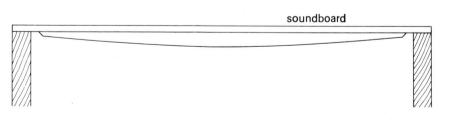

Fig. 64 Shape of rib.

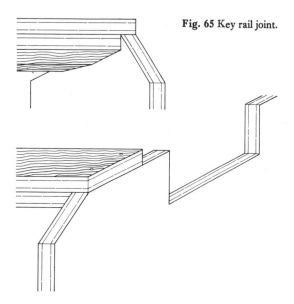

Fig. 65 Key rail joint.

fitted with its front edge 7 mm from the front end of the soundboard, between the dampers and the jacks.

The hitch-pins.

A line is drawn across the hitch-pin rail, 4 cm above the bottom of the floor, and the places for the hitch-pins are marked on it, in line with the grooves in the nut. The holes for the pins are drilled $\frac{1}{16}$ in., sloping downwards towards the front. The one-inch nails used for the hitch-pins should be the thickest which will pass through the holes in the barrels on the ends of the strings. If they are

much thinner they will bend. They will need to be tapped firmly into their holes. The outer ones, being very near the ends, are liable to split out unless the holes are drilled deep enough. There is less risk of this happening if the external side pieces have been well glued in place before the holes are drilled (see Figs 51 and 52).

Varnishing

This should be done next, before fitting the wrest-pins, tuners or strings. When the whole box has been trimmed and smoothed, it can have two or three coats of clear polyurethane varnish, each one rubbed down when thoroughly dry.

The wrest-pins and fine tuners

These are made exactly as described in Chapter 5 for the coke-hod dulcimer. Brass screws and washers, and plated wing-nuts, should be used if obtainable. Failing this, a smear of grease or oil will help to postpone corrosion; so also will regular use of the instrument.

The positions for the holes should be pricked with a sharp pointed implement before drilling. They are then drilled to a depth of 15 mm, perpendicular to the soundboard, using a $\frac{5}{32}$ in. drill. If the holes seeem too tight for the threads, they may be enlarged very slightly by continuing to turn the drill for a while, with no downward pressure, or else by using an $\frac{11}{64}$ in. drill. Another way is to insert and rotate a screw of abrasive paper.

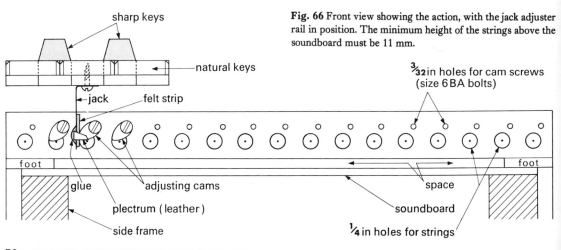

Fig. 66 Front view showing the action, with the jack adjuster rail in position. The minimum height of the strings above the soundboard must be 11 mm.

All strings of the bass psaltery, except for the five shortest, will need $\frac{1}{4}$ in. bolts, in $\frac{7}{32}$ in. holes, for their fine tuners, with wide enough slots to take the thicker strings.

Stringing

The effect of stringing an instrument in different ways, using various gauges and tensions, is not always what one might expect. It is quite simple to design a frame and to string it in such a way that the tension on all the strings is the same. The bridge would be mathematically curved to suit the sounding length of strings all having the same gauge, in which case the length would be doubled for every octave towards the bass. Alternatively, a rectangular instrument could be made, whose strings were graded in thickness from treble to bass, all sounding their correct pitches at the same tension. Instrument makers have long since decided on a compromise, as the most practical solution.

A form of monochord can be made for testing the pitches of strings of various gauges under the same tension. Instead of anchoring the string at both ends, one end is passed through a screw-eye, and over the edge of a table or bench. A bucket of weights is hung by a strong wire hook, threaded through a loop in the end of the string. Weights are added until the prescribed pitch is reached, at a sounding length of, say, 70 cm. If a standard set of steel guitar strings is tested like this, it will be found that they are not all equal in tension, when tuned in the normal way on the guitar. If they were graded for equal tension, the tone at certain pitches would be inadequate. This is partly because the acoustical properties of soundboards, sound boxes and frames are not consistent throughout the range of pitches required of them.

When deciding on a stringing plan, stability of tuning has also to be borne in mind. The strings on a wooden frame stand in tune better if they are reasonably tight, than they do if too slack. They also sound better, but one has to beware of distorting the frame, or breaking the strings.

From all this it will be evident that the best way to string an instrument, while predictable to some extent, must be found partly by experiment. Many factors are involved, the analysis of which would require sophisticated scientific equipment. The only alternative is experience gained through trial and error, by which our predecessors learned to manage extremely well.

An attempt to solve the problem for players of steel strung guitars has been made through the marketing of 'custom gauge' strings, which are stocked by some of the more specialized music shops. These cost more than standard sets of strings, but they do enable the enthusiast to experiment with many small variations of gauge and tension.

The stringing layout suggested here is based on standard gauges, and will work quite well with even the cheapest strings. However, there is no doubt that the tone in certain parts of the compass will be improved if intermediate sizes are used. For those who care to experiment, the best way is to begin at the highest note, with the thinnest top E string available, and to go on using that gauge until the tone starts to become 'wiry' or 'twangy', when the next thicker gauge is due.

Sometimes one finds the treble, or shorter end of an instrument strung with one string for a pair of notes, turns being taken round the hitch-pins to prevent the tuning from slipping. This has the obvious disadvantage that if one string breaks, both have to be replaced. A better way is to cut the string in half, using the barrel on the end of one part, and making a new loop on the other.

The loop is made as follows: double back about 2·5 cm of the end, squeezing it tightly round a one-inch nail. Grip the two parts together in the vice, leaving most of the loop projecting. Twist the nail, stretching the loop away from the vice, until a tight spiral has been formed. It will unwind a turn or two when released. If twisted too many times, the string will break. If too few, it may unwind itself again. The right amount is soon learned by experience.

The soprano psaltery can be strung entirely with high E, or first, steel guitar strings. Nine, of standard length, should be sufficient, if they are cut in half.

For the alto psaltery, the nine shortest strings will be guitar seconds, (B); the next six will be thirds, (G); and the four longest, fourths, (D).

For the bass, the shortest five will be guitar

fourths, (D); the next seven, fifths, (A); and the longest seven, sixths, (E).

Each string should rest in an extremely small notch on the top of the bridge. A single light touch with the corner of a triangular file is enough. The strings can be accurately positioned, one at a time, as they are fitted, making sure that they all run parallel to each other, and to the sides of the instrument. The tension of the strings should be increased a little at a time, evenly over the whole instrument, until they are about a tone below their eventual pitch. The fine tuning, which is described later, is left until everything else has been completed.

Making the keyboard

The sprung part, or 'comb', is marked out on a selected piece of 4 mm gaboon plywood, with the surface grain at right-angles to the keys. If it went the other way, the touch would be very springy and unpleasant. The measurements need to be copied carefully from Figs 59 and 67. Notice that the length of the keys, from the back of the key rail to the front of the plywod part, is 20 cm. The width of the board will obviously depend on the number of keys in the particular instrument which is being made.

The board is sawn 5 mm bigger all round than its eventual size, and is then screwed in place on the key rail, using $\frac{1}{2}$ in. No. 4, round-headed, brass or chromium wood-screws, with washers. It will be seen from Fig. 67 that there are two screws to each key. To ensure accuracy, the board can be pinned in position before the screw holes are drilled. A panel pin can be put part-way in at each end, where two of the holes are to be drilled, and replaced by screws in the other holes when their turn comes. The holes are drilled through into the key rail to a depth of 11 mm from the top of the keys, using a $\frac{1}{16}$ in. drill.

The board is then removed, and a piece of spare wood is clamped or pinned under its holes, to prevent splintering, while they are enlarged to $\frac{5}{32}$ in. This is just enough to allow a small amount of sideways adjustment at the front ends of the keys, when they have been separated.

The next thing is to screw the board to the key rail at its outer ends, being careful not to over-

tighten the screws; and to check that its outer edges, as marked, are exactly in line with the outer edges of the psaltery. Amend the lines if necessary; remove the keyboard, and plane its edges down to size. Do not yet saw the individual keys.

The naturals

The cutting and glueing of the naturals is made easier with a simple jig, something like a tray with two of its edges missing. Its base is a piece of 6 mm plywood, 30 cm square. Two straight strips of wood, at least 1 cm thick, are nailed along adjacent edges of the plywood to form an 'L', the inside of which is exactly a right-angle. One of these strips will be used to line up the fronts of the keys, while the other rests against one side of the keyboard. A line representing the back edge of the key rail is drawn on the base of the jig, so that the total length of the keys, to the fronts of the naturals, will be 26 cm. The plywood keyboard is then screwed in position on the jig, with one screw at each side.

The naturals are 12 cm long, and are cut from strips of hardwood 23 mm wide and 6 mm thick, with their ends all carefully squared on the shooting-board. They are put in their places in the jig, with a strip of 4 mm plywood under their front ends to keep them on a level with the top of the plywood part of the keyboard. If the naturals are the correct width, and the keyboard has been drawn accurately, the lines between E and F, and between B and C, should coincide. If they do not, amend the drawing on the keyboard accordingly.

Before going any further, the letter name of each natural, and its numerical position, should be written underneath its front end.

We are now ready to saw the keys as far back as the front edge of the key rail. Remove the board from the jig, and support it, the right way up, over the edge of the bench. Use a very fine saw, held obliquely, and without obvious pressure. Any slight splintering which may occur will then be underneath, where it will not show. The saw cuts should be made along the centres of their lines, not to one side or the other. Do not cut any further back than the line of the front of the key rail, which is 3 cm from the ends of the keys, until after the key coverings have been glued on.

Having completed the sawing, replace the

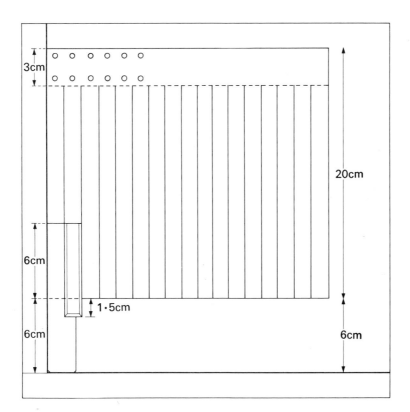

Fig. 67 Keyboard for bass or soprano psaltery in position in its jig for glueing on naturals and sharps before sawing into separate pieces.

keyboard in the jig, with the naturals in their correct order. Draw a line across the naturals, 4·5 cm from their front ends. This marks the length of the pieces to be cut out for the sharps. The width of these pieces is marked from the saw cuts in the keyboard. It is a wise precaution to put a cross on all the pieces to be cut away, thus avoiding the extreme frustration of discovering that you have carefully sawn off the wrong piece. Remember that the notes D, G and A will each have to have two pieces removed.

For sawing, the naturals can be held between strips of wood in the vice. Use a fine saw, keeping close to the line, but not cutting into it. The final cuts into the corners need especial care, since the appearance of the keys will be spoiled if they go too far. After sawing, the edges can be trimmed with a chisel.

When this has been done, a fine shaving must be removed from both the outer edges of all the

naturals, on the shooting-board, so that their front or widest ends will not rub against each other.

The front corners will look better when seen from above, if they are slightly bevelled. This can be done with a chisel, or a fine file. A further refinement, mainly decorative, and therefore optional, which is sometimes seen in old instruments, is to chamfer the top edge of each side of the naturals, for a distance of about 3·5 cm from their front ends.

By now the keys should fit in their places like the pieces in a well made jig-saw puzzle. The next step is to glue them to their other ends. Here is a simple way to do this without using clamps. Scrape a few shallow grooves in the underneath of each natural where it is to be glued. Beginning with the lowest note, apply a thin coat of Evo-Stik Resin W Woodworking Adhesive, and place the key in its position in the jig. Having made certain it is correctly lined up, press down hard on the glued area

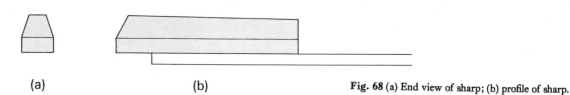

with your thumbs, for about half a minute. Let go carefully, and do not disturb that key again for at least three hours. Do the same with each successive note, taking care to preserve the narrow gaps between them, and to align the back ends, and the fronts, correctly, before applying any pressure. Do not use an excessive amount of glue, as it will squeeze out and weld the whole keyboard together.

The sharps

Now is a good time to put the jig on one side, and concentrate on making the sharps. Having decided on the wood, the method of cutting them will depend on its thickness.

The base and soprano psalteries each have seven sharps, while the alto has eight. They are 7·5 cm long, 13 mm to 13·5 mm wide at their bases, and 15 mm high. Allowing for saw cuts, as many as eight sharps can be cut from a single piece of wood which is 13 cm across the grain, 7·5 cm with the grain, and 15 mm thick. Although they can quite well be made from thinner strips, it is easier to give them all the same profile when they are cut from one block. A suitable shape is shown in Fig. 68 (see also Fig. 51). Notice that the sides of the sharps slope inwards a little towards the top, to allow more space for the fingers between them. The fronts slope backwards from the level of the naturals, and the tops slope very slightly downwards towards the back ends, although whether they do so or not is a matter for preference.

If the sharps are cut from a single block, the profile can be shaped all at once, by planing across the grain with a sharp and finely set plane. Make sure the block remains rectangular from the back and front views. When the individual pieces have been sawn out, allowing about 1 mm spare width, the sides can be sloped inwards, by planing them against a bench stop, with the plane slightly tilted. To ensure symmetry, mark the amount of wood to

be removed with pencilled lines, and check the progress at frequent intervals.

Each sharp is fitted individually, by planing its base to the exact width of its key. It should then be smoothed with fine abrasive paper, care being taken not to round its edges and corners too much. The method of glueing the sharps in place is exactly as for the naturals. Finally, the entire keyboard may be treated with a liberal coating of linseed oil and allowed to dry.

However many keyboards you may eventually make, whether simple ones like this, or fully pinned, bushed and weighted, there is always a feeling of genuine satisfaction, and eager anticipation of music to come, when the sharps begin to appear in their places among the naturals. Even if your first attempt is rather less than perfect, you may surely be excused a little self-congratulation when looking at it.

The damper blocks

A strip of 9 mm plywood, 12 mm wide, is glued under the keyboard, across all the keys, with its back edge 12 cm from the fronts of the naturals. This is sawn through from above, using the original saw-cuts as guides, to form the blocks into which the dampers will be screwed.

It is now time to separate the keys from each other, keeping to the lines already started. Each key should first be clearly numbered underneath, since it will only fit properly in its original position. Any roughness, or surplus glue, should be carefully removed from the edges of each one, after sawing.

The damper blocks are chamfered on the side away from their screws, as illustrated in Fig. 51 (see also Figs 53 and 56). If this is not done, it will be impossible to remove adjacent keys, when their dampers have been fitted.

The jacks

A simple jig, as shown in Fig. 69, enables all the

jacks to be made quickly and accurately. It consists of a carefully squared strip of wood, 10 cm long, 1 cm wide, and about 6 mm thick. Panel pins are pushed through two $\frac{1}{16}$ in. holes near one end, and an $\frac{1}{8}$ in. stud is fitted near the other end. The exact position of the pins and the stud are important. The stud can be made from a piece of an $\frac{1}{8}$ in. bolt, or a nail of suitable thickness, and tapped into its hole.

The weather strip to be used is cut into pieces 12 mm wide and 35 mm long, with one corner removed, as described for the model of the action. A piece of the metal is laid along the angle of a bench hook, with its longer (unwrapped) edge against the stop. The pinned end of the jig is then placed exactly on top of it, so that its end is level with the narrower end of the jack. The pins are tapped lightly with a hammer, thereby punching the centres of the two holes in the jack. The one at the narrow end is drilled $\frac{3}{32}$ in. and the other one, for the plectrum, $\frac{1}{8}$ in.

The $\frac{1}{8}$ in. hole is then placed over the stud at the other end of the jig, and the narrow end of the jack is bent squarely over that end of the jig. The direction in which the end is bent will obviously depend on which way up it is placed on the stud. Fig. 69, and the action model, should be studied carefully before deciding which is the right way. If some jacks are bent the other way, the resulting chaos, when you try to put the parts together, will resemble that caused by a few guardsmen turning left on parade when all the others turn right.

The plectra

The easiest and most economical way to cut these is from a strip of suitably tough and hard leather, 1 cm wide and 3 mm thick. Wedge-shaped pieces, tapering from 4 mm to a point, are chopped in alternate directions, as shown in Fig. 70, using a Stanley knife, a razor blade or a sharp chisel. The final trimming is done after they are glued in place as described in Fig. 55 for the model of the action. The exact shape of each plectrum has a marked effect on the tone of the instrument.

If you are unable to find any leather hard enough to produce a good tone, a small quantity of glue, spread on the top surface of the plectrum, will help to stiffen it. Beware of overdoing this, however, or

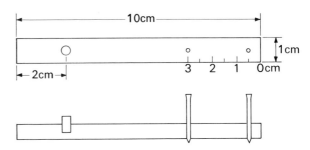

Fig. 69 Jig for drilling and bending jacks.

the tone will become harsh, and the adjustment difficult.

The dampers and adjusters

These are also made as already described (see Figs. 56 and 57), and screwed into their holes. Remember to glue small strips of felt to the jacks where they slide on the guides, otherwise the action will click unpleasantly.

Assembling

The front key rail should be covered with two or three layers of thin felt (or one thicker), to a depth of 3 mm, when compressed. This, together with the correct adjustment of the dampers, should give a touch depth of approximately 7 mm.

The action is assembled beginning with the highest note and working down the scale. Each key should be made to work before the next one is screwed on. Time and trouble spent in doing this will save endless unscrewing and replacing of keys later, with consequent enlarging of screw holes, which may then have to be plugged.

Points to note in regulating the action are:
(a) The height of the dampers, to obtain a level keyboard.
(b) The tension of the springing of the jacks against the adjusters, resulting from the amount they are bent at the top. (The minimum possible, as long as contact is made, will ensure a quiet and easy action.)

Fig. 70 Plectrum cutting.

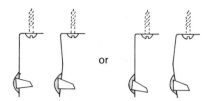

Fig. 71 Plectrum adjustment.

(c) The angle, height and cut of each plectrum in relation to its string. A plectrum which slopes up or down too much can be corrected by slightly bending the jack, as shown in Fig 71. In the released position, the plectrum must just have re-passed the string.

(d) The cam adjustment, affecting the extent to which the plectrum overlaps the string, and hence, touch-weight, tone, loudness and key return.

(e) The tightness of the locking nuts of the cam screws. If these are slack, the adjustment in (d) above will not remain set.

(f) The spring of the keys, which can be regulated with packing pieces if necessary. The minimum required to ensure return of the plectrum when the key is released very slowly, will result in a pleasing touch. If the design has been followed accurately, no adjustment should be needed. However, if a key 'winds', i.e. twists in its length, a packing piece can be glued under one edge of its mounting, to level its front end.

It is also important, when tightening the key screws on the mounting rail, to align the front ends of the keys so that they are all equally spaced, and not rubbing against each other.

Tuning

The tuning of instruments with wooden frames is subject inevitably to variations of temperature and humidity. In this respect the wing-nut tuners on the psalteries are a great asset.

To start with, they should only be tightened enough to prevent their washers from rattling. The strings are then tuned fairly accurately, by turning the wrest-pin bolts with a large screwdriver. The nuts which help to support these bolts should be finger-tight on the wood. Any tendency for a wrest-pin to unwind can be countered by tightening its nut still further. From now on, the fine tuners can be used, until they reach the limits of their slots, when they will have to be unscrewed again, and the wrest-pins turned a little more.

Equal temperament

As already mentioned, this involves the division of the octave into twelve equal semitone intervals, or steps. The simplest way for beginners to achieve this is by comparing each note with its equivalent on a well-tuned piano.

When two notes are slightly out of unison, a 'beat' effect is heard. The closer the pitch of the notes, the slower the beat. When the unison is perfect, the beat will disappear altogether. This effect also occurs with other intervals, particularly thirds, fifths and octaves; a fact which is made use of in equal-tempered tuning.

For the non-musician, it should be explained that an 'interval' is the distance in pitch from one note to another. Thus a perfect fifth would be the theoretical distance from C to G, inclusive, or from D to A, or in fact any interval of that order. Similarly, a perfect fourth would be the theoretical distance from C to F, or from F to B flat, and so on. A major third is such as would occur in a major scale, from its key-note to the next but one above; say, from C to E. 'Octaves' are notes having the same letter name in different parts of the keyboard.

Equal temperament is based on narrowed fifths, wide fourths, and even wider major thirds, which become wider still, the higher they are in the octave being tuned. An easy way to learn to hear beats is to tune the octaves on the psaltery. Having established a beatless octave, about half a turn of one wing-nut will introduce fairly slow beats, and their speed will increase as the wing-nut is turned further. Remember that turning clockwise will sharpen a note, and vice versa.

Next, the fifths can be tried. Their beats are almost as easy to hear as those of the octaves. We are, of course, listening for *perfect* fifths, such as C and the G above, or D and the A above. These encompass the letter names of eight adjacent semitones, if you include the lowest and highest notes. It is no use sounding the notes separately,

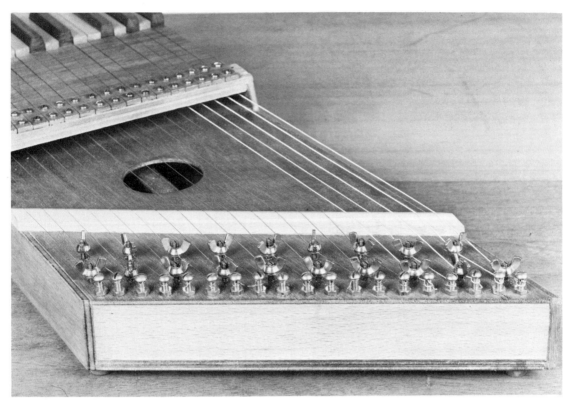

Fig. 72 The tuning end of the alto keyed psaltery showing the wrest-pin, bolts, fine-tuners and bridge.

Fig. 73 Alto keyed psaltery with nearest key and front rail removed. The adjusting cam can be seen in position.

Fig. 74 Alto keyed psaltery complete. The rib and the centre framing strut are just visible through the hole in the soundboard.

and relying on melodic instinct. The better this is, the more it will tend to lead away from equal tempered tuning. The two notes must be sounded *together*, for the beats to be heard.

Perfect fourths, which encompass six adjacent semitones, inclusive, as for example, C and the F above, or F sharp and the B above, are more difficult to hear. They sound weird when far out of tune, but it can be difficult to decide when they are just right.

The beats of wide major thirds are rapid, seeming full of nervous energy. Beatless major thirds, on the other hand, sound calm and peaceful.

The easiest of the psalteries to tune is the alto, since it is just large enough to be done entirely by fifths and octaves. If any two, or all three, are being tuned together, all the other notes can be tuned by octaves from the alto.

Tuning the alto psaltery

The first thing is to establish, from a piano, chime-bar, tuning fork, or whatever source is available, a pitch for the A above middle C, as a starting point, or 'bearing'. When that is done, tune the lower A, an octave below it, eliminating any beats.

The rest sounds simple enough. Success depends on narrowing the fifths just enough, but not too much. It will require some patience at first, but as in all things, skill comes with practice.

Remember to make *all* the octaves beatless, and *all* the fifths very slightly narrow. The sequence is as follows: the low A up a fifth to E; B down an octave to B; B up a fifth to F sharp; F sharp down an octave to F sharp; F sharp up a fifth to C sharp; C sharp up a fifth to G sharp; G sharp down an octave to G sharp; G sharp up a fifth to D sharp; D sharp up a fifth to A sharp; A sharp down an octave to A sharp; A sharp up a fifth to F; F down an octave to F; F up a fifth to C; C up a fifth to G; G down an octave to G; G up a fifth to D; D up a fifth to A.

If this is done successfully, the last fifth, from D to A, will sound about as narrow as all the others. If there is a rapid or violent beat at this point, do not be tempted to alter the A again, but have another try at narrowing all the fifths, until the right amount is learned. It becomes much easier when the sequence has been memorized.

Tuning the bass and soprano psalteries

The naturals can be tuned in fifths and octaves, as follows: low C up a fifth to G; G up a fifth to D; D down an octave to D; D up a fifth to A; A up a fifth to E; E down an octave to E; E up a fifth to B; low C up an octave to C; C down a fifth to F.

We now have a slight problem; how to relate the sharps to the naturals. The more orthodox way, but uncertain for beginners, is to tune F sharp a slightly wide fourth below B and proceed in fifths and octaves from there. A less orthodox, but perhaps easier way, is to sound the common chord E, G sharp, B; adjusting the G sharp to obtain the smoothest possible sound. The pitch of the G sharp is then raised until fairly rapid beats begin to be apparent. Again, experience is the best guide. The remaining sharps are tuned as follows: G sharp down a fifth to C sharp; G sharp up a fifth to D sharp; D sharp down an octave to D sharp; D sharp up a fifth to A sharp; low C sharp up an octave to C sharp.

Tuning the psalteries, with their wing-nut tuners, can become an absorbing and harmless pastime, since it does not loosen the wrest-pins. On no account, however, should success with the psalteries tempt the enthusiast to have a go at the piano, for the tuning of which years of training and experience are needed. There is vastly more to it than merely listening to beats and twiddling nuts. Even some inexperienced professional tuners can ruin good pianos.

A finishing touch

Until, or unless, a case is going to be made to contain all three psalteries, a useful addition to each one is a board across the front, with a rail by which to pick the instrument up without risk to the key fronts. It is easily made from three pieces of wood, as shown in Fig. 74, and is attached by two screws, so that it can be removed for adjustments to the action. It also helps to fit four small rubber feet under the soundbox. This increases the resonance from below, when the psaltery is stood on a table.

A clavichord action

A model, similar to the one for the harpsichord-like action of the psalteries, can be made to demonstrate the simple operation of the clavichord. No damper is needed, as the string is permanently damped at its hitch-pin end with a piece of cloth or felt. Instead of a jack, there is a tangent, which can be made from a $\frac{3}{16}$ in. brass bolt, with the head removed, and the end filed to a screwdriver-shape. The other end is screwed into a block glued to the underside of the key, where the jack would otherwise have been. When the key is pressed, the tangent touches the string, sounding a very quiet note, as described on p. 57. A touch depth of about 5 mm is sufficient.

Simple as this is, to make a good clavichord is far from easy. So gentle a mechanism needs a soundboard and a case of high quality and resonance, to produce a satisfying sound. Brass strings, two per note, are best for the lower and middle ranges, although steel is often used for the higher notes.

The sprung keyboard used for the psalteries would be quite suitable for a clavichord, with the tangents working the reverse of the normal way up. Perhaps there is an opportunity here for readers with an experimental turn of mind to explore further the possibilities of resonance and tone-production, using the kind of materials described in this chapter. A clavichord would need careful designing, to ensure the utmost reduction of all impediments to the tone, such as heavy casework, or strength where it is not needed. The soundboard and its supports would need to be slender, and the bridge, as well as the ribs, clear of its edges. The strings, which might be somewhat lighter than those of the psalteries, could run obliquely, from the fronts of the keys towards the farther right-hand corner, enabling the instrument to be of the traditional rectangular shape, but with a soundboard considerably larger than is possible in a normal clavichord.

Early this century, Arnold Dolmetsch begun the revival of the family of keyed psalteries—the clavichords, spinets, virginals and harpsichords—which had been so thoroughly ousted by the arrival of the pianoforte at the end of the eighteenth century. This revival has now grown into quite a large industry, with many excellent makers in Britain, Europe and America, often adapting modern materials to traditional designs. There is also a growing number of enthusiastic amateurs, building their own instruments.

It may be that readers who have had the patience and enthusiasm to follow step by step the making of the simple keyed psalteries described here, will now want to go further, and try their hand at making a larger and more orthodox instrument. There are many excellent and fascinating books on the subject. The following are particularly recommended:

Zuckerman, W. J. *The Modern Harpsichord*, Peter Owen, London (1970).
(To which the author is indebted for the tuning sequence of the alto psaltery)
Hubbard, F. *Three Centuries of Harpsichord Making*, Harvard University Press (1965).
Russell, R. *Harpsichord and Clavichord*, Faber & Faber (1959).

Index